Achieving QTLS

The Minimum Core for
Numeracy:
Knowledge, Understanding
and Personal Skills

Achieving **QTLS**

The Minimum Core for
Numeracy:
Knowledge, Understanding
and Personal Skills

Sheine Peart

First published in 2009 by Learning Matters Ltd

British Library Cataloguing in Publication Data
A CIP record for this book is available from the British Library.

ISBN: 978 1 84445 217 0

Cover design by Topics – The Creative Partnership
Text design by Code 5
Project management by Deer Park Productions, Tavistock, Devon
Typeset by PDQ Typesetting Ltd, Newcastle under Lyme
Printed and bound in Great Britain by Bell & Bain Ltd, Glasgow

Learning Matters Ltd
33 Southernhay East
Exeter EX1 1NX
Tel: 01392 215560
info@learningmatters.co.uk
www.learningmatters.co.uk

Mixed Sources
Product group from well-managed
forests and other controlled sources
www.fsc.org Cert no. TT-COC-002769
© 1996 Forest Stewardship Council

Contents

The author

Sheine Peart

Sheine Peart is a lecturer in post-compulsory teacher training at Nottingham Trent University. Before this she worked at South Nottingham College for 15 years, teaching numeracy to learners on a wide variety of vocational programmes, and managing the college's teacher education programmes. She has broad experience of practical classroom issues and extensive experience of working with learners who present challenging behaviour. She is currently engaged in doctoral research on the experience of Black male learners in the post-compulsory sector.

Acknowledgements

To all my family and friends – thank you for everything.

The author and publisher would like to thank the following for permission to reproduce copyright material: the Institute for Learning.

Every effort has been made to trace the copyright holders and to obtain permission for the use of copyright material. The publisher and author will gladly receive any information enabling them to rectify any error or omission in subsequent editions.

Introduction

This book has been written for all tutors in the lifelong learning sector. You could be currently studying to gain a recognised teaching qualification, you may have been working in the sector for some years and are already qualified, or you could be interested in extending or updating your own professional knowledge. This book is not just for numeracy tutors or those who need to demonstrate how they are developing the numeracy skills of their learners, although these tutors should find the book of interest. The appeal of this book is wider than this, and will be useful to all tutors in addressing the numeracy needs of their learners, or for any tutor who has asked themselves questions like 'Why does the mention of number work seem to fill my learners with dread? How can I work with my learners to help them through this? What is dyscalculia? Why is number work relevant to my subject area? What number development opportunities should I be seeking as a tutor in the sector?' These are significant questions and there is no pretence you will find the answers to these questions within the pages of this book. However, the book will assist you in engaging with these issues and will help you work towards ways in which you can begin to produce your own working solutions to these concerns.

This book is not principally a theoretical text, although there is reference to the work of others, but is a support to help you work through some of the issues associated with number skills and number work. In each chapter there are a number of different exercises. These are designed to engage you, the reader, in a series of thought-provoking exercises, so you can consider the matter in some depth and begin to demystify some of the associated issues. In places it is suggested that you may wish to work with colleagues or talk to other related professionals. This may be particularly useful if you are exploring a new topic or area.

Finally it is important to appreciate that this book will *not* teach you how to become a mathematician. That would require far more work than could reasonably be expected within the constraints and scope of this book. However, it will help you to develop your own skills and to work with your learners to develop their skills in the context of your own subject.

Lifelong learning and teaching qualifications

Lifelong Learning UK (LLUK) has produced the overarching professional teaching standards for all tutors working in the post-compulsory sector. These standards set out the skills, knowledge and qualities needed by tutors in the sector. In addition to these generic standards LLUK has also identified and described *the minimum core in ... mathematics expected of all teachers in the sector* (LLUK, 2007, p2).

The Institute for Learning (IfL) is the body responsible for licensing tutors to work within the post-compulsory sector. Two different levels of recognition exist:

- Qualified Teacher Learning and Skills (QTLS) – these are tutors with full recognition status and whose role *carries the full range of teaching responsibilities and requires the teacher to demonstrate an extensive range of knowledge, understanding and application of curriculum development, curriculum innovation or curriculum delivery strategies* (IfL, 2008, p24). These tutors will hold a Diploma in Teaching in the Lifelong Learning Sector (DTLLS), or its equivalent at level 5 or above;

- Associate Teacher Learning and Skills (ATLS) – this role *carries significantly less than the full range of teaching responsibilities* (ibid) associated with QTLS. These tutors will hold a Certificate in Teaching in the Lifelong Learning Sector (CTLLS), or its equivalent at level 3 or 4.

All tutors, regardless of whether they hold full or associate status, are expected to provide evidence of holding the equivalent of a level 2 numeracy qualification and to be able to support learners in developing their numeracy skills at an appropriate level.

How to use this book

The title chapters of this book relate directly to the knowledge, understanding and personal skills needed by tutors identified in 'Addressing literacy, language, numeracy and ICT needs in education and training: defining the minimum core, 2007', and to the continuing professional development (CPD) requirements described by the IfL. Each chapter can be read as a separate individual article, although forming part of a composite whole, and is therefore linked to the other chapters of the book.

The organisation of each chapter is the same. Each chapter begins with a set of objectives which identify the learning outcomes of the chapter. Links to the minimum core numeracy as specified by LLUK are then described, followed by professional standards relevant to the chapter. Particular links to CTLLS and DTLLS qualifications are also given. It has not been possible to provide generic links to the Certificate or Post/Professional Graduate Certificate in Education, as each awarding institute determines these individually. However, this book will also be useful to those students studying for such qualifications, as the ability to demonstrate competence in numeracy will feature in these qualifications as well.

Within each chapter there are different case studies, practical and reflective tasks. These are based on real-life experience and provide a context for the work. You may recognise or have personal experience of some of the situations described. At the end of each chapter there is a learning review audit which will allow you to self-assess your own understanding of the issues covered in the chapter. Finally you will find a list of the references used, suggestions for further reading and a list of useful websites. Please do not consider this to be an exhaustive list of sources. There are many others and it is likely that you will know other equally useful references.

This book has been written to try and unravel some of the mysteries associated with numeracy and to try and make some difficult ideas, accessible and meaningful. It is meant to provide a framework for positive reflection and practical activity. It is intended to be useful to all tutors in the sector – trainees, existing practitioners and those returning to study – in progressing their own and their learners' knowledge, skills and understanding of number.

REFERENCES   REFERENCES   REFERENCES   REFERENCES   REFERENCES

IfL (2008) *Licence to practise: professional formation – your guide to qualified teacher learning and skills (QTLS) and associate teacher learning and skills (ATLS) status.* www.ifl.ac.uk

LLUK (2007) *Addressing literacy, language, numeracy and ICT needs in education and training: defining the minimum core of teachers' knowledge, understanding and personal skills.* London: LLUK

Websites
www.ifl.ac.uk Institute for Learning
www.lluk.org Lifelong Learning UK

1
Continuing professional development

By the end of this chapter you will be able to:

- explain the importance of continuing professional development (CPD) to practitioners within the lifelong learning sector;
- describe own levels of knowledge, skills and understanding in relation to numeracy;
- determine short-, medium- and long-term personal number development needs;
- identify possible future personal progression routes in number which will help you support your learners' experience.

Links to minimum core numeracy

This chapter relates to the following minimum core standards:

A2   Develop personal numeracy knowledge and reflect upon own experiences

      Identify own training and development needs

Links to Professional Standards

AS4   Reflection and evaluation of own practice and continuing professional development as teachers

AS7   Improving the quality of practice

CP 3.4   Ensure own personal skills in literacy, language and numeracy are appropriate for the effective support of learners

Links to Diploma in Teaching in the Lifelong Learning Sector (DTLLS)

Unit 5   Continuing personal and professional development

Note: The Diploma qualification only requires that numeracy is integrated into the first three mandatory units (Planning and Enabling Learning, Enabling Learning and Assessment, and Theories and Principles for Planning and Enabling Learning). However, unit 5, a later mandatory unit, provides the most appropriate opportunity to specifically integrate developing personal and professional skills.

The nature of being a professional

This remains a contested and hotly debated subject, and there is no one single agreed definition that describes being a professional tutor within the lifelong learning sector. In many ways this is not surprising as professionalism and being a professional are continually evolving concepts, and the nature of a developing debate is that it is unlikely there will be universal agreement. Indeed it may even be a fool's errand to seek this. However, unless some notion of professionalism can at least be suggested, it becomes impossible to engage with, or extend the debate. For this reason, it is important to formulate some broad concepts of what being a professional in the lifelong learning sector could mean.

Being a professional is informed by a myriad of features. A helpful initial definition of being a professional is someone who works in those *occupations where practice is underpinned by a body of discipline-specific (as well as generalist) knowledge and where principles and professionalism, including ethical behaviour and a service orientation, provide the foundation for professional practice* (Higgs and Titchen, 2001, pix). Central to this definition is the

3

idea that there is a core of information, related to an area of practice, that professionals should possess and would need to develop (possibly through a period of intense study in higher education) prior to entering the profession. Furthermore the definition also requires that professional behaviour should be informed by principles and ethics. While not specifically defining such principles the proposal that professionals should work for the benefit of clients, in a service-orientated manner, suggests that professional behaviour should be informed by the concept of 'doing good' for a broader community.

The IfL, the body responsible for conferring QTLS and ATLS, has published a *Code of Professional Practice* which identifies the behaviours required of tutors working in the lifelong learning sector. Many of these behaviours are similar to those identified in the previous definition. The code stipulates six behaviours which it expects all its members to demonstrate. These are:

- professional integrity – towards learners, colleagues, institution and the wider profession;
- respect – for learners and colleagues in accordance with relevant legislation and organisation requirements;
- reasonable care – to ensure the safety and welfare of learners;
- professional practice – to comply with Institute CPD policy and guidelines;
- disclosure – to notify the Institute of any criminal engagement;
- responsibility – to comply with the Institute's conditions of membership.

(IfL, 2008b, p1)

Again the idea of service, this time to learners, other tutors and the sector, is clearly articulated. The *Code* further develops this concept by including the notions of respect and care. Importantly the *Code* specifically requires that members *act in a manner which recognises diversity as an asset and does not discriminate in respect of race, gender, disability and/or learning difficulty, age, sexual orientation or religion and belief* (IfL, 2008b, p2). This is an important difference between the IfL's understanding of professionalism and the earlier definition given. Here is an open and clear signal to members to behave in an anti-discriminatory fashion and, by implication, support and uphold values of equality and justice.

The evolving nature of employment is also recognised, by obliging members to engage in ongoing development, recognising the constantly changing environment of the lifeling learning sector. Further the *Code* introduces two new concepts, of criminal disclosure and responsibility towards a professional body. As there are many young and sometimes vulnerable learners in the lifelong learning sector, there is strong justification for the first of these two new ideas. The second idea, that of responsibility towards an autonomous industry collective, is well established in other professions, for example, law and medicine, and as such it is logical that the IfL should also make this demand of its members. However, it is significant to note that neither within the IfL's *Code of Professional Practice*, guidance for professional formation nor guidelines for continuing professional is there any express mention of principles or ethics to guide and inform professional behaviour. It may be that ethical behaviour is taken as an assumed norm for all education sectors including the lifelong learning sector; however, it could be questionable whether it is prudent to make this assumption.

A further difference between the IfL's guidelines and those of some other professions is that although the IfL acknowledges the importance of subject-specific knowledge in other policy documentation, it makes no requirement for such knowledge to be formally accredited through qualifications. The only mandatory qualifications specified by the IfL are an approved teaching qualification and evidence of literacy and numeracy qualifications at or above level 2. This could be recognition that many tutors in the lifelong learning sector have developed knowledge through practical experience and lack formal qualifications. However, it does raise a noteworthy conundrum of which area is perceived to be of greater value by the IfL – subject-specific knowledge or teaching knowledge? This position initially appears to be at odds with the Further Education Teachers' Qualifications (England) Regulations 2007, which state that those wishing to hold QTLS or ATLS should have a *specialist's subject qualification approved by the Secretary of State* (DIUS, 2007, paragraphs 5.1b and 6.1b). However, as holding such qualifications is only required *where the Secretary of State has decided that such a qualification is necessary* (ibid), it appears both the IfL and central government are unwilling to make subject-specific qualifications a prerequisite for working in the lifelong learning sector.

PRACTICAL TASK PRACTICAL TASK PRACTICAL TASK PRACTICAL TASK PRACTICAL TASK

Obtain a copy of the IfL's *Professional Formation* document. This can be downloaded from the IfL website. Familiarise yourself with the mandatory and personal elements necessary to apply for QTLS or ATLS. Which of the elements do you feel confident you will be able to satisfy? Are there any areas where you feel you may need further training? Although you will need to complete all elements stipulated in order to make an application for QTLS or ATLS to the IfL, what is your own view of the value and the necessity of each of these components?

The context for continuing professional development

The lifelong learning sector is, arguably, the most diverse of all education sectors. It includes *teachers, trainers, tutors, lecturers and other teaching professionals* (IfL, 2008b, pp3, 4) who work in *traditional learning settings, such as colleges and institutions ... 'offsite' contexts ... or work-based or community learning*. It is a dynamic, fast-changing and responsive sector that endeavours to meet the needs of individual learners, whole communities, employers and government. Moreover, through a commitment to national learning targets and by delivering a comprehensive and flexible education package, the sector aims to contradict the adage that 'you can't be all things, to all people, all of the time'. Furthermore the sector is seen as being *at the centre of providing opportunities for lifelong learning, and a means of promoting economic growth, social cohesion and social justice* (Jephcote et al, 2008, p164). Within this context, it is not only desirable that you, as a staff member working in the sector, update your skills but is essential if you hope to be able to keep up with the changes within and demands of the sector.

One of the principles involved in obtaining and retaining QTLS or ATLS is you will engage in a process of CPD throughout your career and should engage in a minimum of 30 hours' professional development activity each year in order to retain your licence to practise. Although this is now clearly stated as a professional requirement, it is important to remember that professional development is not a new invention created by the IfL for the purposes of obtaining QTLS or ATLS.

Good practitioners who were interested in the welfare and development of their learners and in ensuring they delivered the best possible learning experience have always engaged in a process of continually updating their personal skills base. Indeed prior to the introduction of QTLS, ATLS and the IfL, many employers had already developed a process of annual staff development, where staff in discussion and negotiation with their manager(s) would identify the most appropriate development opportunities for tutors to complete. These discussions sometimes, although not necessarily, occurred as part of a formal appraisal system and would often be captured in a personal development portfolio, where all past and planned future activities were recorded. For these employers the introduction of a prescribed system of ongoing professional development can be seen to be a formalisation of an already existing system. Even without such an employer-formulated framework, many individuals made the decision to actively engage in their own development and regularly produced personalised development plans.

The various factors influencing the current context for CPD are usefully summarised in a *model of dual professionalism* produced by the IfL (2007, p5; Figure 1.1).

Figure 1.1 Model for dual professionalism

This model recognises the challenges of accommodating subject-specific and pedagogic knowledge, and introduces a third dimension of policy context. This third element is significant, for although an understanding of both your own subject and teaching and learning are necessary to successfully work in the sector, the actual development you choose to engage with will most likely be determined by *a consideration of the context in which you work* (IfL, 2007, p5), for it is this context which will signify the most urgent development priorities.

PRACTICAL TASK PRACTICAL TASK PRACTICAL TASK PRACTICAL TASK PRACTICAL TASK

Complete a review of the development activities you have engaged with over the past 24 months. Which of these were specific to your subject and which were informed by pedagogy? How significant was your own particular policy context in determining the activities you completed? What opportunity did you have to integrate other *personal* development activities which are not recognised in the IfL's model into this schedule?

REFLECTIVE TASK

Consider the model of dual professionalism produced by the IfL. What influences do you believe to be most significant for your own development? Are there any other influences you think should have been included in this model? How could you use this model to help you plan your own CPD? What is the significance of funding to your planned CPD? How does this model take account of the work/life balance?

A rationale for CPD – a practitioner's perspective

After completing your formal teacher training, (a mandatory requirement of obtaining QTLS or ATLS) you might have been (or could currently be) looking forward to a quieter time, which is not punctuated by the need to complete assignments, be observed, take part in presentations or other assessed activities. Indeed it is not uncommon to hear some tutors say how relieved they were/are to put their textbooks away and 'get on with the real business of teaching'. However, *the days when initial training in a profession was regarded as sufficient to last an entire working life have long gone* and it is now necessary to regularly *up-date your knowledge, skills and attitudes in every aspect of your work* (Gray et al, 2001, p228). Moreover such a narrow view of initial teacher training fails to appreciate the true scope of the programme, and while having completed an intense period of training it is understandable that some tutors may have such feelings, they belie a principal focus of teacher training and the real aim of professional development.

Teacher training courses are not solely for the purpose of enabling you to apply for QTLS or ATLS. More importantly, these programmes lay the foundations for you to become a reflective practitioner who views ongoing professional development as being at the heart of your own, and by inference your learners', development. *Teachers cannot stand still once they have finished their teacher training courses* and *teacher training is often just the beginning of a much longer process of activity and study that will continue in the workplace* (Tummons, 2007, p34) and throughout your working life. It is through engaging in this process of continuing and continuous development that you graduate from being a trainee or self-taught practitioner to being a professional tutor, able to self-diagnose and identify your own development needs.

In much the same way, it could be claimed, people graduate to being adults by taking responsibility for their own actions, taking ownership of your own development can be said to be a defining characteristic of becoming a professional educator. Professionals do not need to be directed to undertake training activities, for *self-motivated professionals (can) be expected to seek out the development (they) need* (Wallace, 2007, p82). Professionals are able to recognise the value and the worth of different actions and can select activities which are productive, useful and meaningful to complete, often engaging in passionate debate about the significance of various programmes.

By undertaking such a proactive stance to professional development, lifelong learning tutors can ensure that they stay engaged with the knowledge, processes and procedures associated with their own subject area, the minimum core and in wider educational arenas. It is this investment of energy, emotional and intellectual labour that allows tutors to remain passionate about learning and teaching, and in turn, to impart this enthusiasm to their learners.

CASE STUDY

The following vignettes illustrate two different tutors' attitudes towards CPD, one at the start of their career and one part-way through their career. After reading the two vignettes try to:

- locate each practitioner in terms of the IfL's dual-professionalism model;
- decide what sort of development opportunities each practitioner appears to value the most;
- identify any contradictions or anomalies you can see in each of their stories;
- determine what practical issues engaging in CPD raises for each of these tutors;
- establish what benefits each practitioner has gained by engaging in development activities.

Cameron

I did the full-time pre-service PGCE last year and I was glad to finish it. All that theory and stuff – I was happy to see the back of it. On top of that I also had to do a level 2 numeracy test, as I got a D at GCSE. I thought that was a bit rich – it's not as though I signed up to teach maths. I was really pleased to get this job and get back into my subject – the thing that I most want to do. I was even pleased that they said I would have a mentor for the first year, someone who knew their stuff and could guide me on the recent developments in the field, although I was a bit concerned that I felt I wasn't trusted enough to be left alone and needed to be baby-sat. I'm not too sure about the idea of mentors. They seem to come in two sorts – over-enthusiastic energetic types, or tired old sages who feel there is nothing new to learn. I know that has to be nonsense as the field is changing all the time, and if you've lost your passion for the job how can you pass anything on? Anyway, all my mentor wanted to talk about was a new model of peer education that they were developing in the college. Peer education? More like collective peer ignorance. How can those that don't know anything teach each other? Surely that is our role as tutors? We are the experts, the ones that know. I don't know why they couldn't have found me a couple of day courses offered by the awarding bodies or something like that and let me get on with finding out more about my subject. That would have been far more use to me, cost the college less money and waste far less time.

Neema

I finished my teacher training a few years ago and only now do I feel that some of the things we learned make sense. Maybe my head was too full when I first started teaching to try and do the things that I had been taught, and maybe I was more concerned with just surviving those first years and keeping my sanity. I had heard some of the old guard talk about initiative overload, but I didn't really believe it until I started to live it. There is just so much stuff arriving all the time that I sometimes wonder how I can keep up with it all. So, when my head of department asked me if I wanted to take part in the subject learning coaches programme, I wasn't keen. It's not that I don't want to learn, I know how useful the Cert Ed has been, it's just that I didn't know how or where I would find the time to fit it in. Anyway, I said 'yes' in the end. Then I had to make provisions for the classes I was going to miss. I was able to set up cover work for some of them, but for others it was just too critical to miss the sessions so I ended up negotiating to teach them at another time, so that they didn't lose out. That was difficult – I tried to explain that although it might feel inconvenient, it was better than not having a session at all.

I have just finished the second module of the coaches' programme and I am really enjoying it. I didn't realise how easily and how quickly you can lose touch with ideas; and how easy it is to slip into bad habits. Meeting up with others, learning together and then testing ideas out back in the college has been a whole new way of learning for me. It's not like when I did the Cert Ed. Now I know stuff, but I don't know it all. There is still room for more learning and room for more development. One of the best things about the programme is I now have a network of colleagues in other colleges who I can share ideas with and test out my thoughts before trying them for real. I've also met up with people outside of my area, and we have talked about literacy, numeracy, social justice and all sorts. We are even considering some sort of tutor exchange across colleges. I never knew learning could be like this and none of this would have ever happened if I hadn't taken the time to get involved.

A rationale for CPD – a college management perspective

Following the 1992 Further and Higher Education Act, all colleges became independent businesses, in charge of all aspects of their affairs. Once colleges were firmly located in a market-driven environment in which they had to compete with other colleges for business, a clear business objective was necessary to provide training. Potential reasons for employers offering training opportunities to tutors might include to:

- be satisfied that the workforce has an up-to-date understanding of the subjects they deliver in order to provide the best possible experience for learners;
- address a current skill shortage for individual employees or the collective workforce;
- increase staff effectiveness;
- tackle an area of poor work performance;
- reduce staff turnover and employee attrition rates;
- improve employee satisfaction;
- enhance the institution's reputation as a good employer;
- enable the establishment to obtain a recognised industry standard such as Investors in People.

Whatever the reason for providing staff training, once colleges were run as businesses, managers needed to see a tangible return for any training offered. And, within a market-driven economy, managers were likely to want the greatest possible return for the smallest possible investment. Because of this, employers and employees may not always hold the same views on how or what development opportunities should or could be completed. An employee, for example, may wish to attend a taught numeracy refresher course to update their skills. While this would address an identified training need, it might not be possible to release an employee to attend such a course or to locate the funds necessary to pay for the course. An employer might prefer a tutor to complete a self-directed online learning programme which could be undertaken outside standard working hours. This would achieve the same learning objective and cause minimal disruption to the workplace.

As there is no agreed standard procedure for delivering development opportunities within the sector, individual employees may find that they need to engage in separate negotiations with their manager(s) when determining what training could be undertaken and how this should be completed. Furthermore, it is likely these negotiations will need to be completed on an annual or more frequent basis.

CASE STUDY

The following case study provides one head of department's perspective on CPD in very particular circumstances. Once you have read the case study try to:

- pick out the issues involved in this situation;
- decide where you think this approach fits into the IfL's model of dual-professionalism;
- identify how else this situation might have been managed or how would you recommend handling the situation;
- decide what the individual tutor responsibilities are in this situation.

CPD – a head of department's perspective

The consultant's report on the key skills numeracy team has just arrived. In many respects it just confirms many of the things I feared. They don't work as a team, they don't plan lessons, work is poorly marked or not at all, and they all seem too keen on talking about other tutors in front of the learners rather than focusing on the needs of our students. I can't ignore information like this. I have talked with the Vice-Principal and we have decided to put a four-point action plan into place. This will involve:

- each member of the team, within the next four weeks, being observed by one of the college's senior managers;
- all members of the team having a full appraisal with me in the next six weeks;
- an audit of all schemes of work and lesson plans to be completed by the Quality Assurance department;
- a full review of all marking schemes and associated documentation to be completed by the staff team;
- a full-day team-building event with myself and one of the Vice-Principals to draw members of the department together.

What can be counted as CPD

Tutors working in the lifelong learning sector need to engage in training and development to ensure that they *keep up-to-date, in the context of a rapidly changing work environment* (Rothwell and Herbert, 2007, p121). While this is not contestable, there is the further question of *what this updating might be* (p121), and furthermore who decides what could be included in such a programme.

There are no hard and fast identified 'routes' laid down for … professional development (Armitage et al, 2006, p37) and the previous case studies and your own experience will tell you many different activities can count as CPD. Professional development is essentially about you, your subject knowledge, your understanding of teaching and your working relationships with learners and other professionals. As you are central to the CPD process and as you have the best understanding about what your individual needs are, you should, ultimately, decide what can be counted as relevant CPD. This is confirmed by Wallace (2007, p82) who suggests that *as reflective practitioners we are able to identify for ourselves the areas of practice which need development*.

However, as has been observed earlier, it is not only your view which determines which CPD activities occur, and there are a variety of different and sometimes competing influences. In the final analysis, much CPD often represents a compromise of views, values, beliefs, available funds, the constraints of time and in the end what is achievable and feasible within any given resource base. Nevertheless, it is helpful to have some understanding of the types of CPD that regularly occurs in the sector. Such activities include:

- attending accredited courses or programmes related to teacher development;
- peer review and peer observation;
- work shadowing;
- team teaching;
- carrying out and disseminating action research;
- engagement in structured professional dialogue/learning conversations;
- membership of committees, or steering groups related to teaching or your subject area;
- partnership activities with other colleges, employers or other providers;
- visits to community organisations;
- returning to study;
- line-management appraisal;
- self-evaluation of your own teaching practice.

(adapted from IfL, 2007, p9)

This is not an exhaustive list of all possible CPD activities, but it provides a useful starting point when considering which activities you could be purposefully involved in.

Numeracy and CPD

All teachers need to be confident in working with colleagues to ensure the development of ... numeracy ... skills of learners (LLUK, 2007, p2) and teachers working in the lifelong learning sector are required to hold a mathematics qualification which is at *least equal to that demanded of learners in the national curriculum for schools* (LLUK, 2007, p61). This point is further emphasised by the Department for Innovation, Universities and Skills (DIUS) who have determined that tutors in the lifelong learning sector should have *obtained such an award as may be approved by the Secretary of State, for the purposes of demonstrating that a person has the necessary ... numeracy ... skills to teach* (DIUS, 2007, paragraphs 5.1c and 6.1c). If you do not already possess an award at this level, it is now essential that you obtain such a qualification.

Numeracy skills audit and personal numeracy development plan

It is helpful to have a clear understanding of your personal numeracy skills. Full details of the range of numeracy skills you may need are provided in 'Addressing Literacy, Language, Numeracy and ICT Needs in Education in Education and Training: Defining the Minimum Core of Teachers' Knowledge, Understanding and Personal Skills, 2007'. Although it is mandatory that you hold a numeracy qualification which is at least equivalent to a level 2 standard, you may find in practice, that you need a far higher skills level. Even if the programmes you teach on do not require a skill level beyond level 2, it is your professional responsibility to ensure that you are able to work competently, effectively and confidently at this level.

The following framework provides a structure for you to self-assess your numeracy skills, to identify areas for further development and to plan your personal progression in numeracy. This framework may not precisely match your individual personal circumstances, but it does allow you to focus in some detail on what development might be required to consolidate or improve your current skills base.

Numeracy skills audit		
➢ Numeracy credentials	Level	Date obtained
• stand-alone numeracy qualifications – record any accredited numeracy programmes you have successfully completed • embedded numeracy skills – record any numeracy work you have completed which has been part of another programme • non-accredited numeracy experience – record any other numeracy work you have completed in the past		
➢ Self-assessment of competence The following processes, identified in 'Addressing Literacy, Language, Numeracy and ICT Needs in Education in Education and Training' represent a range of skills that it is advisable for tutors working in the lifelong learning sector to possess		

Skill	Level of competence			
	1. High	2. Good	3. Adequate	4. Needs developing
• Understanding positive and negative numbers of any size • Completing calculations • Understanding fractions, decimals and percentages • Understanding ratio and proportion • Knowledge of properties of 2D and 3D shapes • Understanding of area, perimeter, volume and capacity • Ability to manipulate discrete and discontinuous data • Understanding frequency diagrams, pie charts and scatter diagrams • Working with money, metric and imperial units • Understanding probability • Understanding and using units correctly • Estimating and approximating • Ability to use a calculator				
➤ Personal numeracy development plan				
From the list of skills provided, and considering the programmes you work on, which skills are priority areas for you to develop over the short, medium and long term?				

Table 1.1 Personal numeracy skills audit

Possible numeracy development routes

There are a variety of dedicated numeracy qualifications that you may wish to consider taking to further develop your skills. These include both accredited and non-accredited programmes, offered by a range of awarding bodies and higher education institutions. Below is an indication of the sort of programmes you may wish to consider. This may be a sensible topic to discuss with your line manager(s), or a colleague in the human resource management (HRM) department. However, as new programmes are being developed all the time you will need to check what is currently available in your area.

Accredited qualifications	Key audience	Qualifications available
Level 2 qualifications	These are suitable for practitioners who have not yet obtained a recognised accredited level 2 qualification. This is the basic minimum-level qualification required of all tutors working in the lifelong learning sector, even if you are *not* teaching on programmes at level 2.	• GCSE maths • Key Skills level 2 • Basic Skills level 2
Level 3 qualifications	This the minimum recommended qualification level required for anyone delivering a level 2 numeracy programme.	• A level maths • Key Skills level 3
Level 4/5 qualifications	These are specialist qualifications for tutors who have chosen to mainly deliver numeracy courses.	• Degree-level programmes • SfL level 5 Numeracy

Non-accredited qualifications	Key audience
Levels are not always allocated to non-accredited programmes	These programmes are suitable for any tutors wishing to consolidate or update their skills. There are a variety of national development opportunities offered by the Quality Improvements Agency (QIA), Skills for Life Improvement Programme (SfLIP) and the National Centre for Excellence in Teaching Mathematics (NCETM). Details of these programmes are available on-line. Other programmes could be offered on a local or regional basis. This information may be held centrally by your HRM department.

Table 1.2. Development routes for tutors

A SUMMARY OF KEY POINTS A SUMMARY OF KEY POINTS

CPD is no longer a desirable optional extra, but an essential requirement for all tutors employed in lifelong learning and an expected sector standard. This chapter has reviewed:

> the nature of professionalism in the sector;

> the contextual framework for CPD;

> a range of different perspectives regarding CPD;

> a variety of activities that may be counted as CPD;

> some of the numeracy development opportunities you may wish to consider.

There is an array of perceptions concerning CPD – some consider it a threat, others see it as an opportunity, some an inconvenient nuisance, others still as a chance to make a real difference to their learners' experience. In some regards, these perceptions are immaterial. CPD is now a reality. Perhaps, the most important issue here is how will you in your working life choose to engage with the process?

Learning review audit

Topic	I feel confident in doing this	This is an area I will need to develop
I can identify the significance of CPD for tutors in the lifelong learning sector		
I can describe a range of relevant CPD activities it would be appropriate for me to complete		
I am able to identify my own levels of numeracy skills, knowledge and understanding		
I have considered my own development needs in relation to numeracy		
I know what future actions I need to take to further develop my personal numeracy skills		

REFERENCES   REFERENCES   REFERENCES   REFERENCES   REFERENCES

Armitage, A, Bryant, R, Dunnill, R, Renwick, M, Hayes, D, Hudson, A, Kent, J and Lawes, S (2006) *Teaching and training in post-compulsory education.* Maidenhead: Open University Press

DIUS (2007) *The Further Education Teachers' Qualifications (England) Regulations.* Nottingham: DIUS.

Gray, D, Griffin, C and Nasta, T (2001) *Training to teach in further and adult education.* Cheltenham: Nelson Thornes

Higgs, J and Titchen, A (2001) *Professional practice in health, education and the creative arts.* Oxford: Blackwell Science.

IfL (2007) *Guidelines for your CPD* London: IfL.

IfL (2008a) *Code of professional practice.* Available at www.lfl.ac.uk

IfL (2008b) *Licence to practise: professional formation – your guide to qualified teacher learning and skills (QTLS) and associate teacher learning and skills (ATLS) status.* Available at www.lfl.ac.uk

Jephcote, M, Salisbury, J and Rees, G (2008) Being a teacher in Further Education in changing times. *Research in Post-compulsory Education,* 13: 163–72

LLUK (2007) *Addressing literacy, language, numeracy and ICT needs in education and training: defining the minimum core of teachers' knowledge, understanding and personal skills.* London: LLUK

Rothwell, A and Herbert, I (2007) Accounting professionals and CPD: attitudes and engagement: some survey evidence. *Research in Post-compulsory Education,* 12: 121–38

Tummons, J (2007) *Becoming a professional tutor in the lifelong learning sector.* Exeter: Learning Matters.

Wallace, S (2007) *Teaching, tutoring and training in the lifelong learning sector.* Exeter: Learning Matters.

FURTHER READING   FURTHER READING   FURTHER READING   FURTHER READING

Fawbert, F (ed) (2003) *Teaching in post-compulsory education, learning, skills and standards.* London: Continuum.

Jarvis, P (2006) *Adult education and lifelong learning, theory and practice.* Abingdon: Routledge-Falmer.

Pollard, A (2002) *Readings for reflective teaching.* London: Continuum.

Pollard, A (2005) *Reflective teaching.* London: Continuum.

Websites

www.lfl.ac.uk The Institute for Learning

www.qia.org.uk Quality Improvements Agency (QIA)

www.sflip.org.uk Skills for Life Improvement Programme (SfLIP)

www.ncetm.org.uk National Centre for Excellence in Teaching Mathematics (NCETM)

2
Different factors affecting the acquisition and development of number skills

By the end of this chapter you will be able to:

- **identify wider societal attitudes towards numeracy;**
- **describe the different number skills expected of learners as determined by age;**
- **describe the funding issues faced by adults wishing to return to study;**
- **identify ways in which motivation can affect an individual's development of number skills;**
- **describe the influences of gender on achievement;**
- **understand how socio-economic status and different cultural attitudes can affect achievement in numeracy.**

Links to minimum core numeracy

This chapter relates to the following minimum core standards

A1   Awareness of a range of personal, social and cultural factors including attitudes in wider society, age, motivation, gender, ethnicity, and socio-economic status in relation to numeracy

Links to Professional Standards

AK 1.1   What motivates learners to learn and the importance of learners' experience and aspirations

AK 3.1   Issues of equality, diversity and inclusion

Links to Certificate in Teaching in the Lifelong Learning Sector (CTLLS)

Unit 2   Planning and enabling learning – how to plan for inclusive learning

Links to Diploma in Teaching in the Lifelong Learning Sector (DTLLS)

Unit 2   Planning and enabling learning – how to plan for inclusive learning

Unit 4   Theories and principles for planning and enabling learning – theories and principles of learning and communication in planning and enabling inclusive practice

Attitudes in wider society

Although attitudes towards numeracy in the UK vary, generally they are not positive. While most people appear to recognise that numeracy is a key skill *required at virtually all levels of employment* and provides *empowering skills for the conduct of private and social life* (Smith, 2004, p2), it is viewed as *a demanding subject, in which only exceptionally intelligent people can actually succeed* (Nardi and Steward, 2003, p357). This despondent attitude has transmuted into a *national cultural bias against maths* where *admitting you are weak in maths in English society is a very acceptable thing to do* (Kowson, 2004).

This negativity, coupled with an aversion to engaging with number work, has produced low levels of achievement throughout the adult population and approximately 6.8 million adults have numeracy and/or literacy skills below entry level 3 (Moser, 1999). Furthermore, according to the National Audit Office (NAO) *26 million people of working age have levels of literacy and numeracy below those expected of school leavers* (2004, p1). In 2001 the government, determined to break this *cycle of low literacy and numeracy skills* (NAO, 2004, p1), launched the national Skills for Life (SfL) strategy to improve the skills level of the adult population. This was followed in 2005 by the National Standards in Adult Literacy, Numeracy and ICT, which specified the levels of achievement expected of all adults.

Since 2001 there has been considerable progress in improving the numeracy and literacy skills of the adult population. The government achieved its 2004 target of working with 750,000 low-skilled learners, and it appears it will achieve the 2010 goal of engaging an additional 1.5 million learners (NAO, 2004). While these figures may appear modest in relation to the 26 million learners identified as having low skills, as progress is made it has become increasingly difficult to engage additional learners, many of whom can be described as disengaged 'hard-to-reach' populations. Within this context, the achievements made to date can be described as promising. Unfortunately although many more adults have been successful in gaining numeracy qualifications, this does not appear to have been accompanied by a corresponding positive shift in attitudes towards number.

REFLECTIVE TASK

Do you, or any of your learners, display *the national cultural bias against maths* described by Kowson (2004)? If so, how does this bias manifest itself and what impact does this have on your learning and teaching environment?

Issues related to age

The population of older people in the UK is increasing. A 2000 study by National Institute of Adult Continuing Education (NIACE) indicated that *in 1997, 32% of the UK population were over 50 and 18% were over retirement age*. By 2031 these figures are predicted to rise to 41 percent and 23 percent respectively. Yet, within an educational context there is no agreed definition of the term 'older learner'. Thus, being able to engage in a meaningful discussion of the issues associated with age remains problematic. In an employment context learners may be considered 'older' when they are in their 40s; the University of the Third Age (U3A – an independent self-help organisation supported by the government which provides educational and leisure activities) suggests older learners are between 50 and 75; while the fourth age represents anyone aged 76 and older. In further and continuing education there are significant numbers of learners who fall within each of these age brackets and you are likely to encounter some or all of these groups. Thus, using any of these definitions, it is highly probable you will be working with older learners at some stage.

Despite lacking an adequate means of describing older learners, it is still possible to identify a range of important, interrelated issues associated with numeracy skills and age. These are:

- issues associated with individual capacity and the ability to manipulate and work with numbers as learners grow older;
- issues associated with the changes to numeracy curricula which have occurred over time;
- issues related to how learners' life experiences affect their number skills;
- and finally, how funding opportunities have impacted on learners' ability to access learning opportunities.

REFLECTIVE TASK

Within the groups that you teach, approximately what proportion of your group are 'older learners'? How many of them are over 40, 50 or 75? What issues, if any, has this presented during your planning and preparation or delivery of number sessions? What steps or action have you taken to manage these issues?

Individual capacity

Understanding number and developing number skills is a complex process which is further complicated by the differences between people and their individual capacity to learn. While it is difficult to define which number skills are innate according to age, it is possible to state society's expectations of number skills as determined by age. These are described in the National Standards for Adult Literacy, Numeracy and ICT; the National Numeracy Strategy (NNS) for Key Stages 1, 2 and 3; and the various GCSE syllabi.

The NNS is very clearly linked to age and indicates which number skills should have been acquired by ages 7, 11 and 14. While it is possible to takes GCSEs at any age, these may be considered the expected number skills of a 16 year old, or the minimum level expected of an adult. The only guidelines which are not specific to age are the National Standards for Adult Literacy, Numeracy and ICT.

Before learners can competently, efficiently and consistently solve number problems in a variety of different settings they will need to have understood certain core principles. If learners have not understood these principles, or have an incomplete understanding, it is likely they will become 'stuck' at a specific stage of development and will struggle to progress beyond this.

The ability to count *is one of the first mathematical concepts* (Lawton, 2005, p22) that learners need to understand to enable them to solve numerical problems. Intrinsically related to counting is the ability to use numerals, and closely allied to both of these skills is understanding place value. These three skills are fundamental to understanding the more complicated processes of addition, subtraction, multiplication and division, which are *actually more efficient and sophisticated methods of solving counting problems* (Lawton, 2005, p53). Building numeracy skills can thus be seen to be a cumulative and hierarchical process where a learner needs to understand key principles before they can progress to other higher-order skills.

Most learners, even adults only just beginning to develop their understanding of numeracy, will have some number skills. For adults at the very start of this learning journey, it would be reasonable to expect that they can:

- use mathematical language such as bigger, smaller, more or less to describe proportions and quantity;
- order, sequence and count objects;
- competently use numbers up to 10 and have an awareness of larger numbers;
- demonstrate an elementary understanding of addition and subtraction.

(adapted from Threlfall, 2002, p1)

Only learners with profound, complex and multiple learning difficulties will be unable to achieve these skills.

By the time learners reach 16, and enter adult life, they are expected to have developed number skills which will enable them to operate at the national standard of level 2 in numeracy. Competence at this level is assessed by achieving a GCSE at grade C or above, or by passing the Adult Basic Skills Numeracy test at level 2. At this stage learners are expected to be able to:

- *read and understand mathematical information;*
- *specify and describe a practical activity;*

- *generate results to an appropriate level of accuracy;*
- *present and explain results.*

(DfES, 2005, p19)

However, not all the adult population have yet achieved this level of competence, and it is likely that you will be working with many learners whose skills are somewhere between early number development and the expected national level 2 standard.

It is important to remember that when you start work with your adult learners they will have already been exposed to a variety of number-learning opportunities. As you begin to work with these learners you may be surprised or confused that some adults can apparently be proficient in one skill area, while lacking ability in another more elementary area. This is likely to be caused by a lack of success in understanding certain core principles. For example, learners may be able to correctly answer 8 × 6, yet struggle to perform the subtraction 84 − 37, or to apply their multiplication knowledge to tell you how many eggs there would be in eight half-dozen boxes.

This example needs to be placed in a context. Many older adult learners will have experienced a traditional teaching approach and will have learnt some number information, such as their times tables, by rote. The only requirement of this system of learning is to provide the correct answer to a given prompt, which is rarely linked to a practical situation. Rote learning does not require understanding of concepts or the ability to apply knowledge to different environments. The adult learner who can correctly supply 48 as an answer could be assessed as understanding multiplication processes without understanding the underlying principles involved. Similarly, the difficulty created by the subtraction problem is likely to have arisen from a lack of understanding of place value. Consequently, when the learner is presented with a columnar subtraction, in which it appears they are being asked to subtract a larger number, 7, from a smaller number, 4, unless they can recognise the significance of place value they will struggle to understand how this is possible.

If learners are 'stuck' at a particular point in their development, it is your responsibility as a tutor to address this. To achieve this you will need to take them back to the point at which they stopped understanding and to help them revisit the principle they are experiencing difficulty with. It can be a challenging and painful process for learners to confront their lack of understanding and you will need to be prepared to try a variety of different strategies, including using early number approaches. You may also need to help them unlearn any misconceptions they may have developed about certain principles.

Even if learners have previously enjoyed success studying numeracy, recent research suggests that *at around 50, (the brain) begins to lose the ability to make new connections; and past 70, people find it harder to retrieve memories* (Barnard, 2005). This has significant implications for teaching and learning. First, if a learner returns to education in their later years they may find it much harder to connect their previous knowledge with new information they are being taught. Second, the learner who is over 70 may find it frustrating and difficult to acknowledge that they can no longer remember number facts they once knew. If this is coupled with the information that *attitudes to mathematics becomes less positive with age* (Eddowes, 1983, p20), the challenge of working with the older learner can be seen to be significant. However, despite these potential difficulties it is important to remember that continuing to engage in education produces significant benefits for the older learner, including increasing social networks, helping to maintain physical and mental well-being and may even help to delay the onset of dementia (Alzheimer's society website).

PRACTICAL TASK PRACTICAL TASK PRACTICAL TASK PRACTICAL TASK PRACTICAL TASK

How many older learners do you teach that have yet to achieve their level 2 numeracy qualification? Do any of these learners appear to be experiencing difficulty in connecting new information to existing knowledge or recalling information? What strategies have you explored to address this concern?

Changes to the numeracy curriculum

Mathematics and numeracy curricula have, in common with other subjects, changed over time. To a degree these changes have mirrored larger, national changes which have occurred in education. In 1944 the tripartite system of secondary modern, secondary technical and selective grammar schools was established. The curriculum delivered in each of these schools was predetermined by the type of school. Grammar schools, which catered for approximately 20 percent of the school-age population, prepared their pupils for further study at university or to enter professional occupations. Only these pupils would have had the opportunity to study the more challenging aspects of mathematics. Under the tripartite system the majority of students would have attended secondary modern or technical schools and would have concentrated on a more restricted numeracy curriculum, designed to equip them for the world of work and industry. Many of these schools, grammar, secondary modern and technical alike, would have used a mainly traditional approach to teaching and learning.

The tripartite system was succeeded by the introduction of comprehensive schools, the first of which opened in 1949. Comprehensive education was meant to provide for all learners of all abilities. In reality although it never completely replaced grammar schools, most local education authorities had adopted the comprehensive system by 1975. In contrast to previous ways of organising education, the newer comprehensive schools favoured a more progressive approach to teaching and learning.

The taught curriculum available in schools in the UK has also been heavily influenced by the various examination bodies. In 1918 the first national qualifications, the School Certificate and the Higher School Certificate, were introduced. These certificates were taken at 16 and 18 respectively. It is important to remember that school-leaving age was only raised to 16 in 1973 and many pupils would have left school without any qualifications at all to go straight into work. In 1951 the General Certificate in Education (GCE) examination was introduced. This was offered at two levels: Ordinary or O-level and Advanced or A-level. GCE exams replaced the School Certificate and the School Higher Certificate. GCEs were principally grammar school qualifications, although some local authorities offered their own leaving certificates for young people not taking these exams.

It was not until 1965 that some degree of unification in educational opportunities occurred with the introduction of the Certificate of Secondary Education (CSE). These exams were for students not taking O-levels and catered for approximately 80 percent of the school population. The separate exams, O-levels and CSEs, had different curricula and were popularly perceived as being of different value, with O-levels accepted as the more prestigious qualification. The introduction of comprehensive education brought the two systems closer together and many schools chose to offer both O-levels and CSEs. Full curricula convergence was achieved in 1988 with the introduction of the National Curriculum and the General Certificate of Secondary Education (GCSE). As a result of these changes all students were now entered for the GCSE examination at 16. Originally GCSE maths curricula were divided into three tiers: foundation, intermediate and higher. Learners entered for the foundation tier were grade restricted and could only achieve a maximum D grade at GCSE. Consequently, *the 30 per cent of the age cohort entered for this tier (were) pre-destined to 'fail'* (Smith, 2004, p6). The Smith Inquiry found this to be a *perverse arrangement* (Smith, 2004, p7) and recommended a two-tier system be introduced. This finally happened in 2006, when the GCSE syllabi were revised to a two-tier system that allowed all learners the opportunity to achieve a grade C in mathematics.

As well as structural changes to the organisation of schools and course syllabi there have been significant changes in the way number is taught in schools. While this has been strongly influenced by curriculum changes, it also reflects societal changes regarding education. Table 2.1 below provides a summary of some of these key differences.

	Traditional approaches	Contemporary approaches
Curriculum issues	Emphasis on number facts and basic arithmetic	Curriculum opened up to include a much broader range of topics including percentages, financial literacy etc
	Emphasis on providing the 'right answer'	Emphasis on processes and understanding how calculations are completed
	Less opportunity for many learners to gain recognised and valued qualifications as a result of separate or tiered exam arrangements	Majority of learners provided with the opportunity to achieve the national standard of a level 2 qualification
	Uniqueness and separateness of number emphasised	Cross-curricular links explored and a more holistic approach taken to numeracy
Teaching issues	Learners viewed as passive receptors of knowledge who needed to learn from expert tutors	Learners viewed as having some degree of knowledge and as active participants in developing their own understanding
	Teaching by rote common and learners expected to know information without necessarily understanding principles behind this information	Learners encouraged to understand how and why knowledge has been produced
	Traditionally organised classes with furniture arranged in rows facing the front	Furniture arranged in clusters to encourage group co-operation
	Direct knowledge instruction from tutors	Learners encouraged to explore knowledge through problem-solving
	Teacher-centred methods used	Learner-centred methods employed

Table 2.1 Summary of principal changes to delivering numeracy

While it could be suggested that traditional methods were more common within state education in the past, these methods have not entirely been replaced by contemporary approaches. In many learning environments it is still possible to find elements of both types of approach and individual establishments may oscillate between the two depending on prevailing imperatives and needs. The government itself has also displayed ambivalence to the two systems, at times advocating a 'back to basics' system, while on other occasions promoting a more liberal approach.

There are merits and difficulties for both types of organisation. For example, supporters of traditional education argue that the cross-curricular approach favoured by progressive educators does not allow learners to develop an in-depth subject understanding; and progressive educators suggest traditional learning encourages learners to view numeracy as a collection of disconnected facts rather than seeing patterns. As both systems have positive and more problematic elements, a more useful way to review the numeracy curriculum is to consider which approaches promote success, while recognising the distinct characteristics of each learner. Consequently traditional and contemporary approaches can be used together and many organisations choose to mix these two methods, depending on individual learner needs.

Life experience

As learners grow older and have a wider experience of life they incidentally and organically develop a variety of different number skills. For example, parents and carers develop skills in weights and measures as they plan family meals; decorators develop skills in area and quantities as they calculate the amount of material needed to decorate a room and nurses extend their understanding of temperatures, volumes and time. In a contemporary leisure context most of society now has an awareness of recommended daily intake values for fat, salt and alcohol. All of these skills are number-based and can be used to support learner development. Problematically for numeracy tutors, however, learners do not always acknowledge how the skills they have developed outside of the classroom can be applied within the classroom, and conversely, they do not necessarily recognise what they have learned in a classroom *could have a use, a relevance, outside of the subject classroom* (Noble and Bradford, 2000, p132). This presents a real challenge for tutors who need to find a way to demonstrate the interconnected nature of both classroom learning and other aspects of learners' lives.

Opportunities to make the connections between taught lessons and the outside world may be facilitated with the advent of functional skills, which emphasise how number skills feature in work and day-to-day activities. However, the problem of encouraging learners to bring their personal life experience into a learning environment still exists. It becomes a tutor responsibility to draw out from learners the number skills they use on a routine basis.

You will need to question learners to find out what number skills they need as a childcare worker, a mechanic, a receptionist or in the home. Open-ended independent numeracy projects are helpful for exploring how learners use number skills in different settings, and provide learners with an opportunity to demonstrate their existing competence to their peers.

Issues associated with the funding process

Funding is a key issue for many adult learners wishing to continue their studies in the lifelong learning sector. Funding is not available for all types of provision and is only guaranteed for adults completing a basic skills course in numeracy or literacy or their first full level 2 or level 3 course. While this organisation may enable the government to achieve its target of all learners having a level 2 qualification in numeracy, it does not necessarily support a broader view of education. For example, adults who solely wish to study GCSE maths rather than a basic skills qualification would not be eligible for funding as this is neither a complete level 2 programme nor included in the SfL strategy. Similarly, current funding arrangements would not support an adult who has achieved a GCSE in maths and wishes to study a single A-level in maths. Many adults enter the lifelong learning sector not to study a full programme, but to slowly reintroduce themselves to learning by studying a single subject in which they are personally interested. These learning opportunities are in danger of being eroded and recent changes in funding arrangements have resulted in over 800,000 fewer adults participating in education from 2005–06 (Lee, 2007).

While existing funding provision may have resulted in a recent downturn in the number of adults participating in continuing education, there have been some positive changes to funding arrangements for older learners. Those who wish to study a full level 2 or level 3 programme can now apply for further financial support through the Adult Learning Grant (ALG). This grant is available to adults studying full-time who have an annual income below £19,500 if they are single or £30,800 for couples. In addition to this, adults who wish to pursue higher education courses can now apply for loans for living costs up to the age of 60 and there is no longer an upper age limit for tuition fee loans.

REFLECTIVE TASK

What is the level of participation of older learners in your institution? Have you or any of your colleagues noticed any changes in participation rates in recent times? What strategies has your institution adopted to encourage the continued engagement of older learners?

Motivation issues

Reasons for adults wishing to study in the lifelong learning sector are as many and varied as there are learners. They can be as diverse as wishing to help children with school tasks to simply completing a course for pleasure. Whatever the reason for participating in education, motivation is a key factor in producing successful learning. Motivation can be divided into two basic categories: positive motivators which promote engagement and demotivators which prevent interaction.

Positive motivators

Positive motivators can be further subdivided into intrinsic motivators, which are driven by a need to achieve a personal desire or goal, and extrinsic factors, which relate to a need to gain either a particular reward or to avoid punishment. Intrinsic factors are essentially 'within you', while extrinsic factors may be considered to be part of your external environment. The following two case studies provide a useful illustration of some of these factors.

CASE STUDY – TERRY

Sandra spent years trying to teach elementary arithmetic to Terry, a slow-learning pupil. She claimed very little success, and the boy left school without even a minimum qualification in mathematics. Two years later Sandra came across Terry scoring for a darts team in a pub. They were playing '501', which involved Terry doing calculations such as 501 − (17 + 11 + [2 × 19]) in his head. Terry had no difficulty with this; he could complete such a calculation accurately in seconds. Sandra could barely keep up with him.

She asked him how he had learned to do in his head, in two years, what he was unable to learn how to do on paper in five years. He replied that if he had not been able to score, he would not have been allowed in the darts team; he loved playing darts, 'so I had to learn it, didn't I?'

(Petty, 2004, p43)

Discussion

In this example the opportunity to be part of a darts team provided Terry with the positive motivation that had been missing throughout his school career. For the first time Terry could now see that his social acceptance was dependent on his numeracy skills. His desire to be socially integrated was so strong that Terry was prepared to learn the number skills he struggled with at school to become part of the darts team. Terry's motivation was extrinsic because it was a feature of his environment, socially driven as it was placed in the context of friendship groups and instrumental because Terry's only reason for engaging in learning was to be accepted on to the darts team. While this example is placed in a social situation, similar circumstances could exist within an employment context. In either case it can be seen that the principal reason for learning is one which is outside of the learner and is not produced by some deep-seated desire to become more numerate.

CASE STUDY – ANGELA

Angela was employed at a DIY superstore. She had set shift patterns but also worked additional hours if they became available. Angela has started attending your basic skills numeracy class following a disagreement with her employer. When asked what had happened Angela replied:

I don't mind doing the extra hours, but I don't like to think they are ripping me off. One month they asked me to do all this extra time. I needed a bit more that month as I had quite a few bills to pay, so I said 'yes'. When it got to the end of the month, and I got my wage slip, I didn't think they had paid me enough. I went to see the supervisor, and he told me that I had only been paid time-and-a-half for the antisocial hours I worked on Sundays and over the bank holiday. The other hours were all paid at standard time. He then did some calculations very quickly to show me this and said that by the time all the stoppages had been taken out, that was all I had earned. I couldn't follow what he was doing so I just agreed, but I couldn't help feeling I'd been taken for a ride. I don't want that to happen again, so I decided it was time I learnt how to do sums.

Discussion

Angela's situation is different to Terry's. She does not need numeracy skills for a specific benefit or to be accepted into a social group. Her motivation arises from a *personal* desire that she does not wish her employer to take advantage of her. She now recognises that she needs numeracy skills to help her make sense of her working life and her routine encounters with number. The only way that she can achieve this is by improving her numeracy skills. This is intrinsic motivation, as Angela's need to develop her number skills stems from within her, and there are no defined rewards attached to the development of this skill.

Although both types of motivating factors have the potential to produce desired learning outcomes, extrinsic motivation can be short-lived. Once a goal is achieved or a perceived threat is removed, the willingness to continue with learning ceases. In contrast intrinsic motivation, because it is based on individualised aspirations continues, and can drive the learner on to further achievements.

Demotivating factors

Wallace (2007) suggests there are four principal demotivators. These are:

- fear;
- boredom;
- previous negative experience;
- loss of hope.

For numeracy a fifth demotivator, antipathy, can be added to the list. While this fifth factor is, to a degree, a product of the other four features, it is often the first demotivator identified by learners. Furthermore, this single issue can often prevent re-engagement with numeracy. While loathing of number may be the first problem identified by learners, it is likely to be the last aspects that you can challenge. To support your learners you will initially need to consider the other four demotivating factors and to find ways to encourage participation. This could include using inspirational materials, providing positive feedback, and setting negotiated achievable goals. Only once an appropriate climate for learning number has been created will you be able to help your learners to move forward and to view numeracy more positively. The strategies identified in Chapter 4 on disabilities and learning difficulties related to number, will be particularly useful here.

REFLECTIVE TASK

Consider the learners you currently teach. How would you describe their motivation? How have you come to form this view? What impact have the different types of motivation had on their achievement? Are there any strategies you could employ to try and encourage greater intrinsic motivation?

Gender issues

The issues relating to gender and achievement in numeracy are not simple and have changed over time. Historically girls were completely denied access to number education and in the early 1800s number work was believed to be an *unacceptable part of their education* (ILEA, 1986, p22). Although maths was later included in the curriculum for girls, they studied the subject for a much shorter time and the curriculum focused on their – presumed – adult responsibilities of domesticity and motherhood. In the early 1900s these differences persisted, with girls being *taught a different kind of mathematics from boys, according to their perceived biological, psychological and social differences* (ILEA, 1986, p22). It was only once the 1944 Education Act was passed that girls were able to access a similar mathematical curriculum to boys. Although this Act removed official differences in the school curricula, stereotypical differences in perceptions continued into the latter half of the twentieth century and *girls were persuaded, subtly and openly, that traditionally masculine subjects such as the 'hard' sciences and maths were 'not for them'* (Francis, 2000, p5). As well as being denied opportunities to study mathematics girls were *marginalised and belittled in the classroom, the victims of systematic discrimination from male classmates and the school system itself* (Francis, 2000, p4). Consequently many girls chose to stop studying number work as soon as they were able to. This cocktail of discrimination, marginalisation and self-elected exclusion resulted in many girls failing to achieve any number qualifications while at school and, as a group, they demonstrated significantly lower levels of attainment than their male counterparts. The legacy of this inequality meant that as late as the 1980s girls continued to underperform in maths relative to their male peers.

The introduction of the National Curriculum in 1988 to England, Wales and Northern Ireland meant that for the first time girls were obliged to study the same mathematical curriculum as their male counterparts and were exposed to the same learning opportunities. This change produced a dramatic effect in girls' achievement and by *the early 1990s it became evident that girls' GCSE results in (this) area were improving, and by 1995 they matched boys' achievements in (this) subject for the first time* (Francis, 2000, p6). The popular press has a tendency to present this improvement in girls' achievement simplistically as a role reversal, or as educational gains for girls being achieved at the expense of boys' education. This is a questionable interpretation of the situation. Although girls *now get better GCSE grades in maths* (Brettingham, 2007) with girls achieving a 57 percent pass rate at GCSE for grades A*–C, compared to boys who obtain 55 percent, they *have yet to outperform boys in any* *meaningful way* (Noble and Bradford, 2000, p120). While girls have now exceeded boys' attainment at GCSE in maths, this difference is not sustained and *once compulsory schooling is completed pupils appear largely to revert to traditional choices, with girls tending to choose arts/humanities* (Francis, 2000, p8).

The reasons for girls currently performing at a higher level are not entirely clear. The new-found success has been attributed to a range of factors including:

- a curriculum which places a greater emphasis on coursework;
- a greater use of 'word problems' rather than short calculations;
- a requirement for sustained effort with careful attention to detail.

In contrast it appears that boys adopt a much more active approach to learning and favour *practical work where they are involved in something, not merely 'book learning'* (Noble and Bradford, 2000, p28). Damningly, some researchers have suggested that *many boys may well have been disenchanted by inappropriate lessons, which do not stimulate the girls either* (Noble and Bradford, 2000, p101), and it is this failure to produce a stimulating and relevant numeracy curriculum which has produced an anti-maths culture and the relatively modest levels of achievement in number seen across both genders.

PRACTICAL TASK PRACTICAL TASK **PRACTICAL TASK** PRACTICAL TASK **PRACTICAL TASK**

Examine the seating plan shown in Figure 2.1. All learners in this group have previously studied the subject and are now re-sitting the course to try and gain at least a C grade. Remembering you are now working with adult learners, how could you intervene in this learner-elected seating arrangement to enhance learning?

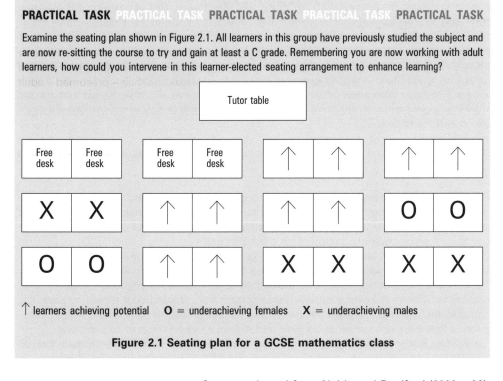

↑ learners achieving potential   **O** = underachieving females   **X** = underachieving males

Figure 2.1 Seating plan for a GCSE mathematics class

Source: adapted from Noble and Bradford (2000, p96).

Socio-economic influences

According to the National Statistics Socio-economic Classification system, there are eight socio-economic groups identified as:

- higher professional occupations;
- lower managerial and professional occupations;

- intermediate occupations;
- small employers and own account workers;
- lower supervisory and technical occupations;
- semi-routine occupations;
- routine occupations;
- never worked and long-term unemployed.

These categories are determined by a variety of factors including employment and income. For convenience they have been condensed into three categories of higher occupations, intermediate occupations and lower occupations, although the general lay person descriptors of upper, middle and working class are still commonly used. Research into achievement and socio-economic group is not specifically linked to numeracy but applies generally to academic achievement across all subject areas.

In recent times more researchers have come to agree that *achievement is hugely influenced by socio-economic class* (Noble and Bradford, 2000, p6) and some researchers even believe that *social class remains the most likely factor to affect one's educational achievement* (Francis, 2000, p11). This second view is not accepted by all academics and some believe the influences of gender and race to be equally important. In very broad terms those from lower socio-economic groups fare less well in the education system and have lower levels of academic attainment than those from more affluent groups. This is not a recent phenomenon and *the British education system has long been marked by sharp inequalities in educational outcomes for different social groups* (Plummer, 2000, p21). This situation continues to this day and recently Strand (2007, p4) found that *pupils in the most deprived schools (35% or more entitled to free school meals) and those living in the most deprived neighbourhoods made less than expected progress*. The outcome of this differential experience is that those from lower socio-economic groups achieve less well in examinations and enter lower-paid and less secure occupations, thus ensuring that class differences are maintained and cemented.

Reasons for differences in achievement, are not universally agreed, but may include the following:

- families from the lower socio-economic groups are faced with hard choices in terms of how they should spend their available financial resources. This could mean that families may need to choose between buying essential household items or purchasing study aids such as books and computers for their children;
- some families from lower socio-economic groups are employed in roles that require them to work shift patterns. A consequence of this pattern of working is that parents and carers may not be available to assist their children with schoolwork;
- some families from lower socio-economic groups have developed a repeating pattern of underachievement where education is not valued or viewed as relevant. A result of this is that there is no attempt on their part to invest in education or to promote academic attainment as important. This has created a cycle of low achievement and has helped to produce a new socio-economic group of the underclass who have never worked or who are long-term unemployed;
- some parents and carers have not, for various reasons, ever acquired appropriate number skills themselves. As such these families cannot offer support to their children and so contribute to a cycle of repeated underachievement;
- many 'better schools' enjoy a high level of home support, which extends to fundraising for the school. Such schools are able to use this additional funding to buy extra resources to use with children in their schools and so encourage even greater achievement.

While these suggestions may apply to some families from lower socio-economic groups they would not be true of all families from this group. To stereotype all families from lower socio-economic groups in this way would be inaccurate. However, it is important to acknowledge there are significant structural inequalities that work against some socio-economic groups and hinder their academic progression.

PRACTICAL TASK PRACTICAL TASK **PRACTICAL TASK** PRACTICAL TASK **PRACTICAL TASK**

Many organisations now collect statistical data which indicates the level of learner achievement by gender, race, age and whether or not learners have a disability. Some organisations attempt to determine the level of achievement by using postcodes as an indicator of socio-economic group. Try to find out what data is collected in your organisation related to socio-economic group and achievement. If nothing is happening, what are the reasons for this?

Ethnicity and cultural issues

Achievement in numeracy varies across countries and cultures. Asian cultures in particular are noted for high academic achievement in number work. This position was confirmed by the *Third International Mathematics and Science Study* (TIMSS) completed in 1995 which recorded the top five performing countries as Singapore, Korea, Japan, Hong Kong and the Czech Republic.

Park (2004) attributed high achievement demonstrated by Asian students to six principal factors:

- a competitive system which values mathematics highly;
- a consistent and simple number system;
- serious student attitudes towards testing;
- regular practice and repetition of learning key information;
- well-qualified maths teachers;
- a cycle of success.

This situation sharply contrasts with Western education. Cockrcroft (1982) reported a lack of sufficiently well-qualified numeracy tutors in schools and colleges, and as late as 2004 this position was still apparent (Smith, 2004). In recent times the government has tried to address the position by introducing a higher level number qualification for basic skills tutors and by encouraging recruitment through offering bursaries and 'golden hellos' to tutors in shortage subjects. However, while these changes have helped to create a better qualified workforce, the benefits of these innovations have yet to fully work through the system.

Although there is competition within the western education system between institutions, this same level of competition is not so evident among learners, many of whom appear to display anti-numeracy, and even anti-education attitudes. The value that is accorded to education in Asian cultures appears to be far greater than that of western cultures, and while Asian youth is apparently characterised by its 'serious attitude towards testing' many learners in western societies choose to disengage with education from an early age. Furthermore, regular practice and repetition only resurfaced as a feature of number teaching in 1999 with the introduction of the National Numeracy Strategy (NNS).

The collective impact of these cultural differences is that in many western cultures the numeracy skills of the population lag far behind those of their Asian competitors. As the global economy evolves and the need for a skilled workforce increases, Western nations are increasingly seeking ways to address this concern and to emulate the success of Asian nations.

A SUMMARY OF KEY POINTS A SUMMARY OF KEY POINTS

There are many different factors which affect the acquisition and development of number skills. This chapter has been used to review a number of these, including:

> how attitudes in society can impact on the development of number skills;

> the influence of age on skills development and retaining information;

> changes to the way numeracy has been taught in schools and colleges;

> how changes in funding have influenced participation rates;

> the ways in which motivation can affect learning;

> the differences in achievement across genders;

> the influence of socio-economic and cultural issues.

While it is tempting to try and attribute the current issues of an anti-numeracy culture and accompanying low achievement rates to one or two of these factors, this would be both oversimplistic and inaccurate. The current situation has been created over a long period of time and represents a complex entanglement of issues. Only a concerted multiagency approach will be able to address all of these issues. These difficult problems will require fresh and innovative solutions which operate on both local and national scales. However, some solutions could be as simple as encouraging learners to acknowledge the number skills *they had previously learned elsewhere ... as actually mathematics* (Noble and Bradford, 2000, p132). By demonstrating to learners the embedded and interconnected nature of numeracy it is conceivable that learners may start to view numeracy as the essential life skill it is, and may be more willing to engage with number work.

Learning review audit

Topic	I feel confident in doing this	This is an area I will need to develop
I have an understanding of prevailing societal attitudes towards numeracy		
I can describe the different number skills expected of learners according to age		
I understand the funding issues facing adults wishing to return to study		
I can appreciate the impact of gender, culture and socio-economic group on developing number skills		
I understand how motivation may influence a learner's development of numeracy		

REFERENCES REFERENCES REFERENCES REFERENCES REFERENCES

Barnard, N (2005) Age does not wither our brains. *Times Educational Supplement*, available at www.tes.co.uk/article.aspx?storycode=2069119.

Brettingham, M (2007) Gender gap yawns wider in schools. *Times Educational Supplement,* 6 July.

Cockcroft, WH (1982) *Mathematics counts: report of the committee of inquiry into the teaching of mathematics in schools.* London: HMSO.

DfES (2005) *National standards for adult literacy, numeracy and ICT.* Norwich: QCA Publications.

Eddowes, M (1983) *Humble pi: the mathematics education of girls.* York: Longman Schools Council.

Francis, B (2000) *Boys, girls and achievement: addressing the classroom issues.* London: Routledge.

Inner London Education Authority (ILEA) (1986) *Girls into mathematics*. Buckingham: Open University Press.

Kowson, J (2004) This innumerate isle. *Times Educational Supplement*, available at www.tes.co.uk/article.aspx?storycode=2033102

Lawton, F (2005) Number, in Henson, A (ed) *Children's errors in mathematics.* Exeter: Learning Matters.

Lee, J (2007) New priorities hit older learners. *Times Educational Supplement*, 6 April.

Moser, C (1999) A fresh start: improving literacy and numeracy: the report of the working group chaired by Sir Claus Moser. Sudbury: DfEE.

Nardi, E and Steward, S (2003) Is mathematics T.I.R.E.D.? A profile of quiet disaffection in the secondary mathematics classroom. *British Educational Research Journal, 29:* 345–67.

National Audit Office (2004) *Skills for life: improving adult literacy and numeracy.* London: The Stationery Office.

NIACE (2000) *Briefing 2000 on learning in later life.* Available at www.niace.org.uk

Noble, C and Bradford, W (2000) *Getting it right for boys ... and girls.* London: RoutledgeFalmer.

Park, K (2004) *Factors contributing to Korean students' high achievement in mathematics.* Available at www.mathlove.com/new3/notice/data/Chap05(kPark0.doc

Petty, G (2004) *Teaching today.* Cheltenham: Nelson Thornes.

Plummer, G (2000) *Failing working class girls.* Stoke on Trent: Trentham Books.

Smith, A (2004) *Making mathematics count: report of Professor Adrian Smith's inquiry into post-14 mathematics education*. London: HMSO.

Strand, S (2007) *Minority ethnic pupils in the longitudinal study of young people in England (LSYPE).* DCSF Research Brief 002.

Threlfall, S (2002) Learning to teach early number, in Frobisher et al. (eds) *Learning to teach number: a handbook for students and teachers in the primary school.* Cheltenham: Nelson Thornes.

Wallace, S (2007) *Getting the buggers motivated in FE.* London: Continuum.

FURTHER READING FURTHER READING FURTHER READING FURTHER READING

Frankenstein, M (1989) *Relearning mathematics, a different third R – radical math(s).* London: Free Association Books.

Berends, M, Lucas, SR, Sullivan T, Briggs RJ (2005) *Examining gaps in mathematics achievement among racial-ethnic groups, 1972–1992.* Santa Monica, CA: Rand Corporation.

Williams, B (ed) (2003) *Closing the achievement gap: a vision for changing beliefs and practices.* Alexandria: Association for Supervision & Curriculum Development.

Websites

www.alg.lsc.gov.uk/ Adult Learning Grant
www.alzheimers.org.uk Alzheimer's Society
www.equalityhumanrights.com Equality and Human Rights Commission
www.niace.org.uk National Instittue of Adult and Continuing Education

3
Barriers inhibiting the development of number skills

By the end of this chapter you will be able to:

- identify personal barriers that may impact upon a learner's development of numeracy skills;
- appreciate how institutional barriers including assessment methods, support mechanisms and internal organisational structures can affect understanding of number;
- identify how different teaching strategies and approaches to learning can influence a learner's development of number skills.

Links to minimum core numeracy

A1   Awareness of personal, institutional and teaching and learning factors that may inhibit the development of numeracy skills

A2   Awareness of the methods and purposes of assessment in numeracy

Links to Professional Standards

AK 4.2   The impact of own practice on individuals and their learning

CK 3.3   The different ways in which language, literacy and numeracy skills are integral to learners' achievement in own specialist area

CK 3.4   The language, literacy and numeracy skills required to support own specialist teaching

CP 3.4   Ensure own personal skills in literacy, language and numeracy are appropriate for the effective support of learners

EP 1.1   Use appropriate forms of assessment and evaluate their effectiveness in producing information useful to the teacher and the learner

Links to Certificate in Teaching in the Lifelong Learning Sector (CTLLS)

Unit 2   Planning and enabling learning – demonstrate knowledge of the minimum core in own practice

Links to Diploma in Teaching in the Lifelong Learning Sector (DTLLS)

Unit 2   Planning and enabling learning – demonstrate knowledge of the minimum core in own practice

Unit 3   Enabling learning and assessment – how to apply minimum core specifications in own specialist area

Unit 4   Theories and principles for planning and enabling learning – how to apply minimum core specifications in own specialist area

Introduction

This chapter will consider the impact of different influences on the development of number skills. Three separate areas will be discussed.

1. Personal barriers.
2. Institutional barriers.
3. Teaching and learning factors.

Each of these three main areas is then subdivided into key issues. The relationship between these areas is illustrated in Table 3.1.

Main area	Key issues
1. Personal barriers	Previous educational experience
	Number skills required
	Language skills required
2. Institutional factors	Assessment processes
	Availability of support
	Organisational structures
3. Teaching and learning factors	Tutor attitude and teaching methods
	Tutor knowledge
	Learners' preferred approaches to learning

Table 3.1 Barriers inhibiting number skills

Personal barriers impacting on the development of numeracy skills

Numeracy and mathematics share a common problem – they are both widely disliked. For some this may even become numerophobia, the irrational and illogical fear of numbers. While this condition is an exceptional extreme, many people readily confess to hating number work and limit their need to engage in this area. The challenge for tutors working with adult learners is to demonstrate the relevance of numeracy and to help them overcome any aversion they may have to the subject. Before you can do this you need to have some understanding of the sorts of personal barriers learners may experience.

Previous educational experience

As a tutor you are often the first person to introduce learners to information or concepts. You are pivotal in developing learners' understanding and shaping their relationship with and attitude towards new ideas. By the time you meet your learners they will have already been exposed to a variety of different learning environments and will have already formed views on the value of certain subjects.

Often learners have had difficult, challenging and *negative experience of learning mathematics at school* (Swain and Swan, 2007, p3). Number has become a subject which they fear and expect to fail in. As fear can be an irrational response based in emotion, it is unlikely learners will be able to specifically identify *why* they did not enjoy the subject and it will be more productive for you to try and uncover *what* aspects of the subject they found most onerous. Such an approach provides greater scope for a more considered learner response and would form a useful part of an initial numeracy assessment.

Possible causes for learners' antipathy towards number could be a result of their objection towards:

- the teacher – was this a personality issue or was it based in the way the teacher behaved?
- the other people in the class – was this everyone in the class or specific individuals?

- the sorts of topics they had to study – were there any topics they found more enjoyable or were all topics equally loathed?
- the technical language used in numeracy;
- being embarrassed at not understanding the work.

Although learners may not be able to tell you why they did not enjoy number sessions, further careful questioning could unearth specific areas of concern. In your role as a tutor it is your responsibility to:

- locate these issues;
- find ways to manage these difficulties;
- help learners overcome any negative feelings they may have about number.

REFLECTIVE TASK

Think about a group you currently teach. How is their attitude to number characterised? Is it generally positive or negative? Through discussion try to discover how and when they developed this attitude. Have any of the reasons suggested earlier contributed to this situation? What approaches have you developed to manage this situation?

Strategies to assist with managing personal barriers

The five areas of concern identified above can be divided into three groups: interpersonal relationships, subject-specific issues and individual concerns. As a tutor you will be able to mediate in many of these areas and begin to address the concerns expressed by learners.

Poor interpersonal class relationships can be addressed by establishing robust ground rules with your learners early on in the programme. Ground rules need to be negotiated by all group members and must apply to everyone *including* the class tutor. Learners who have expressed fears about being made to feel stupid by tutors or other class members will be particularly supported by a ground rule that requires group members to treat everyone in the group with respect. Ground rules cannot necessarily change people's feelings or make individuals fond of each other or their tutors but they can change behaviour and help to establish a supportive atmosphere in which it is clear how the class will work together.

The issue of subject content is a complicated area. Most academic and vocational syllabi are set by external awarding bodies and tutors have very little choice over subject matter. Your challenge as a tutor is *how* to make the subject more enjoyable and accessible to learners. You need to find ways to re-engage your learners by making learning relevant, achievable and fun. No one single strategy will be suitable for all occasions, or for all learners, and you will need to develop a range of different approaches for different contexts to accommodate individual learner needs'. The strategies suggested in Chapter 4 on learning disabilities and difficulties may be useful here.

Numeracy not only assesses learners' ability to complete number problems but also their ability to translate and decode written arithmetical language. There is often an assumed level of language skills which tutors expect learners to use to help them understand and translate numeracy problems. In addition to this learners frequently have been taught to scan read material to gain a general understanding of a subject. While this strategy may be useful in many other curriculum areas, in numeracy it can create real difficulties. Number work requires that learners read information precisely, as failure to do so can easily result in misunderstanding a problem.

The following word problem provides an example of the sort of difficulty that can arise.

Simon works for seven hours on Monday, Tuesday and Thursday, five hours on Wednesday and eight hours on Friday. Each day he takes an hour-long lunch break for which he is not paid. He earns £6.40 per hour. What is Simon's weekly wage?

This problem first of all requires that the learner calculate the total number of hours Simon works each week by adding the daily totals for Monday to Friday together, which are not identical. Learners then need to remember to subtract Simon's unpaid lunch breaks before multiplying the weekly total by £6.40 to determine Simon's weekly wage. A learner who has read this problem quickly may overlook the fact that they need to subtract the lunch breaks and simply multiply the sum of the daily totals including lunch breaks by his hourly rate. Unless the learner has read and understood the problem correctly, they will not complete the correct series of operations. If the learner is in the habit of showing their 'working-out', the tutor will have an opportunity of determining where the learner has misunderstood the problem or made an error. If they are not accustomed to this way of working, locating the difficulty will be harder.

Further issues may be created by the many multi-syllable words associated with numeracy such as diameter, probability and frequency. Some students may be reluctant to ask for help in reading, preferring to struggle with these terms and, not understanding the actual problem posed, risk eventual failure. You can support learners in this area by taking the time to teach the specific arithmetical terms needed and by encouraging learners to produce their own 'numeracy dictionaries'. You can further assist learners by completing an analysis of the reading age of the material you provide. A useful tool for this is the SMOG index (simple measure of gobbledegook) developed by McLaughlin in 1969, which allows tutors to assess the approximate reading age of a given piece of text.

You may not be able to stop learners from feeling embarrassed, but by establishing a positive learning environment in which learners are supported and can achieve, you can help learners to become more confident. Once learners have become confident with number work and feel that they are in control of their own learning, it is likely that their feelings of embarrassment will diminish and their engagement with the subject will increase.

PRACTICAL TASK PRACTICAL TASK PRACTICAL TASK PRACTICAL TASK PRACTICAL TASK

Using a copy of a commercially produced numeracy resource, or one you have made yourself, complete a SMOG analysis of the written text. The formula for this is provided below.

Completing a SMOG analysis:

1. Select your written resource material.
2. Count ten sentences.
3. Count the number of words that have three or more syllables in your selected passage.
4. Multiply this by three.
5. Use the table below to locate the number closest to your answer.

Number of multi-syllable words × 3	1	4	9	16	25	36	49	64	81	100
Square Root	1	2	3	4	5	6	7	8	9	10

6. Find the square root of this number.
7. Add eight to calculate the reading age of the material.

Adapted from National Literacy Trust, available at www.literacytrust.org.uk/campaign/SMOG.html

Numeracy requirements of the programme

The numeracy requirements of programmes are not always immediately apparent. Learners may not realise when they enrol on a course what is expected of them, and can be surprised at the level of numeracy skills needed to participate. For example, students enrolling on a business course may not have expected that they will need to complete a business plan indicating profit and loss forecasts or sports students may not appreciate that they could need to calculate VO2 max measurements for a client.

It is often assumed that learners will be able to manage the numeracy component of a programme and that you as their tutor will have the skills necessary to teach this work. It is important that you feel confident about these demands and that you are sufficiently competent to deliver this element. Most courses will expect learners to be able to apply the four rules of number and carry out routine operations such as addition, subtraction, multiplication and division. Other courses such as construction or science may have additional demands including percentages, data analysis and estimation. To aid tutors some syllabi now provide signposts indicating where there are numeracy demands on the learner, or opportunities for learners to develop their number skills. It is your role to familiarise yourself with these requirements and to make sure your own skills are adequate to deliver this work.

PRACTICAL TASK PRACTICAL TASK **PRACTICAL TASK** PRACTICAL TASK **PRACTICAL TASK**

Complete a numeracy skills audit of your course. What are the number skills required by the programme? What is the current skills level of your learners? What number skills do learners need to develop in order to successfully complete the programme? Which number skills will you need to teach your learners to support their success? What, if any, are the areas *you* need to revise before you can teach your learners?

Language skills

Technical, arithmetical language is an unavoidable subject-specific concern. Numeracy has its own language *and uses a very specialised vocabulary* (Newmarch and Part, 2007, p19). Learners need to be taught relevant numerical terms and you need to be assured that learners understand these terms, knowing how and when to use them. There are no short cuts for this. You may need to give learners word lists of commonly used words or phrases. A helpful format for this is to allocate words to specific functions, thus giving learners further clues on the ways to use these terms. An abridged version of this type of list is shown in Table 3.2.

Cc	Number	Shape	Data	Using number
	capacity centimetres compound	centre circle corner cube cuboid cylinder	charts column count criteria cumulative	calculate centimetre compare consecutive convert

Source: adapted from Henderson (1998, p109)

Table 3.2 An example of commonly used words

Additional complications arise because words often have a precise meaning in a numerical context which may be different to the way the word is used in everyday language. 'Sum' for example does not mean a mathematical problem but is the total of a set of quantities added together. Nor is it the same as the homophone 'some' which means an unspecified quantity.

Average is another example of potentially confusing language, and rather than meaning mediocre is an exact arithmetical term. Further difficulties are created with this particular term because there are three kinds of numerical average: the mean which is the sum of a set of quantities divided by the number of quantities within the set, the mode which is the most frequently occurring figure and the median or mid-range figure. In this case learners are being asked to apply the term correctly and to select the correct term from a choice of three different terms. The difference between everyday and arithmetical language can, for some learners, appear strange and may serve to alienate them even further. When preparing work for learners you need to ensure that the language you use is clear and unambiguous and is readily understood by your learners.

REFLECTIVE TASK

Consider the range of explicit, embedded or implied numerical language for the subjects you teach. Which terms can learners easily understand? Which terms are currently or have in the past created difficulties? What preparation do you need to complete to introduce or explain these terms to your learners?

Institutional factors influencing the development of number skills

Some barriers to developing number skills are a consequence of institutional organisation. Individual learners will not usually have the capacity to influence these factors by themselves and will need your support as a tutor to help them navigate these difficulties.

Inappropriate assessment processes

Effective initial assessment of learning needs is at the core of developing a relevant programme for learners. Accurate assessment is needed so that learners' skills may be mapped against the requirements of the programme. This will help to ensure that learners are placed on a programme in which they can succeed. While learners may begin a programme of study with a lower skills level than is desirable and effective learner support can help to overcome any potential barriers, if the gap between the learners' existing skills and the requirements of the programme is significant, you may need to discuss with learners if they are ready to study a particular programme.

Each individual institution will determine its own entry requirements for courses, but as a general rule, if learners are operating more than two levels below that required by the programme they will struggle to participate. While it may not be advisable to enrol learners onto programmes if they do not have the required skills, it is possible that numeracy may represent a contained area of difficulty and learners have all other skills necessary to participate. This situation is fairly common and in this case you will need to decide if having low numeracy skills would be detrimental to a learner's overall engagement with a programme or if some form of occasional, or specifically targeted support would be sufficient to support their needs.

Time and other pressures sometimes prevent institutions from completing a thorough learner assessment before enrolling students onto programmes, and sometimes may only involve checking a learner's previous qualifications. Although this will probably provide a general indication of ability it cannot provide detailed information of a learner's skills. Alternatively some institutions can be overzealous in terms of entry requirements and request skills which are not absolutely needed for participation. For example, is it necessary that learners undertaking an NVQ level 2 in beauty therapy have a grade C in GCSE maths?

The better and more robust assessment procedures are, the more likely it is a learner will be correctly placed. As numeracy, literacy and ICT are integral features of most programmes, it is important to have a good understanding of a learner's skills in these areas. Colleges and training organisations are assisted here by the range of dedicated assessment tools now available. Examples of some of these are provided at the end of the chapter in the Websites section.

Availability of support

All learners are entitled to choose which college or training organisation they wish to attend and it is the responsibility of organisations to meet the needs of learners. Chapter 4 discusses the range of support available to learners with disabilities and learning difficulties. However, while the Disability Discrimination Act (DDA) places a legislative duty on organisations to make provision for learners who are disabled or who have learning difficulties there is still considerable variation in expertise, understanding and skills across institutions. Furthermore there are other learners who are not covered by the DDA that would benefit from some form of learning support such as additional numeracy classes. There is no single national standard that is applied to all institutions regarding learner support and, to a degree, the quality and type of support available can be a lottery.

Learners who are covered by the DDA should be screened by a member of the student support team or other suitably qualified staff member so their needs can be assessed and appropriate arrangements can be put into place prior to the start of their programme. However, for learners who are not covered by this Act, support needs may only become apparent when a crisis occurs. This could be an internal incident or it might be if a learner fails a module of study. Where initial assessment has been inadequate or does not cover numeracy skills, it is quite feasible that learners may begin a course without fully understanding the number demands of the programme.

This can be a difficult situation for you as a tutor to manage. Your role is not to provide the direct numeracy support needed by the learner but to assist the learner in having their needs diagnosed and then supported. This could involve arranging for a separate screening to determine their numeracy skills or accompanying a learner to an additional numeracy class. It will almost certainly involve you working closely with members of the student support team while the learner's needs are assessed.

Organisational structures that hinder or support development

The nature and type of support available is a key factor in supporting or hindering a learner's skills development. For a learner to be successful in learning the following organisational features need to be in place.

- An established student support team that can cater for a variety of different needs.
- A dedicated core skills team that can help diagnose specific numeracy, literacy or ICT concerns.
- A robust system of assessment that determines a learner's skills level in numeracy, literacy and ICT and assesses a learner's overall suitability for a programme to ensure accurate course placement.
- A mechanism which supports exchange of information between academic, vocational, numeracy, literacy, ICT and support tutors.
- A named tutor who is responsible for tracking and monitoring a learner's progress.

If support is identified as necessary it should:

- be provided in a timely fashion as any delays could hinder a learner's progress;
- be delivered at a time which is convenient and in a fashion which is acceptable to the learner;
- be reviewed at regular intervals with the learner by the named tutor responsible for tracking progress to assess how well the support is working;
- have continuity so that disruption to the learning process is minimised.

If any of these structures or processes is missing, it is likely that learner's progress will be impeded.

The influence of teaching and learning factors

Teaching approaches will have a significant influence on the way learning occurs. Learners often display negative feelings towards numeracy and adopt avoidance strategies. As a tutor you need to ask yourself if the way you have organised your teaching could have, in any way, contributed towards a learner's hostility to number. For example, could there have been any difficulties with:

- the pace of your session – did you provide sufficient opportunity for learners to understand the first topic before progressing onto the next topic?
- the way you asked learners to work – was this individually or in groups?
- the way you presented the work – did you use worksheets, textbooks or interactive type tasks?
- the type of feedback you gave – did this identify learner success and how they could improve or did it solely confirm deficits?
- having a 'slow learners' table – were learners aware you had stratified the class in this way?

As the tutor you have considerable opportunity to make changes to your teaching and the chance to potentially alter how some learners feel about number work.

Establishing a positive teaching framework

As a tutor you decide the pace of learning, direct how learners should work, choose the format in which work is presented, decide how feedback is given to learners and determine whether or not there is a 'slow learners' table. To achieve an optimal learning environment you should base each of these decisions on the detailed knowledge of your learners. You can gather some of this information before the start of the programme when information of learners' previous achievements is supplied, some can be determined from diagnostic assessments and other details will become clear as you develop your working relationship with the group.

Inevitably there will be syllabus pressures and you will need to complete certain course content before assessment points, however, the pace of learning should always reflect the learners' capacity to accommodate information. Even when groups are set according to academic ability there will be a range of *individual needs* (Nardi and Steward, 2003, p359) and there is little merit in 'getting through the syllabus' if it is not understood. Rather than focusing primarily on major assessment points in your teaching, aim to include smaller, more regular assessments. In this way you will know if learners have understood a topic before progressing onto the next area and you can revisit and, if necessary revise, learning goals.

The traditional model of numeracy teaching *is whole class (with) learners working individually through worksheets* (Swain and Swan, 2007, p6). This approach does not allow learners to work *in collaboration with peers* (Nardi and Steward, 2003, p353) or to share experiences. You need to find ways to promote group learning and allow learners to learn from each other. An advantage of this way of working is that learners who are reluctant to disclose their difficulties to tutors are able *to confide in each other* (Chanda et al, 2007, p27) and are often able to develop collective solutions to their problems without tutor intervention, helping to generate feelings of success and confidence in numeracy.

All number work should be supported by high quality resources and there is a variety of well-produced material available. There is no need for you to be dependent on tired textbooks or worn-out worksheets. Online resources can be used to help remove the tedium of endless exercises completed in isolation. The principal limiting factor here is not the availability of resources but institutional budget allocation and the time you have available to create inspiring material.

When giving feedback you need to focus on *the particular qualities* of student work *with advice on what he or she can do to improve* (Black and Wiliam, 2001, p6). You are providing feedback so that learners can develop and you need to be aware of learners' sensitivities. Feedback which creates feelings of embarrassment or failure will not achieve this. Your feedback should identify achievement and direct the learner on how to progress their work.

Finally there is no requirement or need to organise learning in a hierarchical way by establishing a 'slow learners' table. Learners are usually perceptive enough to know that they have been organised into ability groups and may form the view that they lack ability and *this belief leads them to attribute their difficulties to a defect in themselves about which they cannot do a great deal* (Black and Wiliam, 2001, p6). If this should occur it is unlikely that your learners will be motivated to attempt the numeracy work you give them and they will have little opportunity to advance.

Tutor attitude towards and confidence in using number

> *Teachers' attitudes to maths are shaped by their own experiences as learners* (Rowland, 2001).

Your role as a tutor is fundamental in helping students develop their numeracy skills. Your attitude towards numeracy and your ability to use number will be noted by and transmitted to your learners. If you wish your learners to achieve and be successful in their use of number you will need to inspire this belief in them. To achieve this you may first need to revisit your own personal attitude to number and to consider your own thoughts, feelings and experiences of number. Our attitudes towards subjects can be deeply embedded and can have very long and sometimes emotional histories attached to them. It may be difficult to reverse or change these. However, as a tutor you have a professional responsibility to support your learners and to put your own experiences to one side so that you can offer effective support to your students.

CASE STUDY – A TUTOR'S STORY

The following piece of reflective writing concerns a college tutor's thoughts about the start of a new academic year.

Start of year talk from the Principal again. Last year's results weren't good enough so we are all going to have to work extra hard to do something about it. The application of number key skills results were particularly bad and we all need to take responsibility for this. Why do I need to take responsibility? I am not a key skills teacher and they have a tutor for an hour a week to do that sort of thing with them – it's not my job. On top of that my course has been totally revamped. Health and social care used to be about people – all change now. Now it seems the really important thing to be able to do is to read tables and graphs and work out percentages. So now it's become my responsibility to teach them maths. If I don't they won't be able to do the course work and my results will go down. I'm caught whichever way I turn. I was rubbish at maths when I was at school and I did everything I could to get out of it. What am I going to do? I remember when subject knowledge was what counted and you had to know your stuff. All you have to do now is work it out from a table. There's no knowledge in that at all.

Discussion

There are a number of issues raised by this case study. This tutor is clearly concerned about the changes to the curriculum and appears to have formed a view that the situation was better in the past. However, change in education is inevitable. It is not the fact that change occurs that tutors need to discuss, but *how* they propose to implement the changes. This tutor appears not to appreciate that most tutors now have multi-faceted roles and few staff are able to solely concern themselves with subject content alone. Tutors are expected to have personal tutor groups, hold budgets and other additional responsibilities. This tutor's concerns appear to be only about subject content.

The national concern regarding basic skills means that numeracy, literacy and ICT are no longer considered the isolated responsibility of maths, English and computer teachers. This compartmentalised approach to education has not worked for many learners and has been a contributing factor in producing the low skills level evident in the UK today. The life skills of numeracy, literacy and ICT need to be contextualised for learners so that they can appreciate the relevance of these skills. These skills are not now the preserve of the few but are the shared responsibility of many tutors who need to work collaboratively to help improve learners' skills.

REFLECTIVE TASK

What issues does this case study raise? What specific number skills will the tutor in the case study need to focus on for the forthcoming year? What suggestions do you have that would help them introduce these topics to their groups? What should this tutor do about their own concerns regarding numeracy? If you were directed to work with this tutor to produce an action plan to address these issues, what would you include in this plan?

Tutor awareness of number demands of the programme and developing learners' numeracy skills

Because the numeracy requirements of every programme change, you will need to regularly check what these are. As a minimum you should complete this check at least annually, but as course requirements are repeatedly revised by awarding bodies and central government, you may need to carry out this activity more frequently. All learners are expected to achieve the national standard of level 2 in numeracy and you are expected to help achieve this goal by exploiting numeracy opportunities in your subject area. Your responsibilities as a tutor are therefore three-fold.

- To teach the numeracy components identified within your course.
- To support your learners in developing their skills so that they can achieve the national level 2 standard in numeracy, if they have not already done so.
- To determine where in your programme there are opportunities for learners to develop their number skills.

PRACTICAL TASK PRACTICAL TASK PRACTICAL TASK PRACTICAL TASK PRACTICAL TASK

Using an existing scheme of work identify on a session-by-session basis the number skill opportunities within your programme. If it appears there are few opportunities for learners to develop their skills, how could you revise your sessions to include more number work?

Acknowledgement of learners' preferred approaches to solving number problems including informal approaches

If learners do not understand an arithmetical process there is little point in asking 'why don't you understand what I am doing?' If the learner knew the answer to your question they would not be experiencing difficulties and would be able to work out the problems you presented. However, when learners have had concerns they have often developed their own unique methods of problem-solving. While these methods may not be the easiest or simplest of approaches, they are a method the learner understands.

Although there may be a more efficient algorithm to solve particular problems, it is important that *you* recognise the learner's personalised problem-solving approach. You need to be able to understand *what* the learner is doing, *how* the learner's method works, *why* they have chosen this method and the *success rate* of this method. For example, when presented with the calculation 32×15, rather than insisting learners use a traditional pen and paper method to solve this problem, be prepared to accept that some learners may find it easier to work out 5×2, 5×30, 10×2 and 10×30 and then add the products of these four separate calculations together to reach a final figure. While this approach may take slightly longer it is not wrong and it clearly demonstrates the learner has a good knowledge of place value, understands how to partition numbers and can carry out simple multiplication. If the learner's method has a good success rate, is efficient in terms of time and effort and can be universally applied, you will need to be confident that there are *significant* benefits for the learner swapping to another method. Only if the learner's method is unsuccessful, laborious and has limited use should you consider imposing an alternative algorithm. In numeracy there can be more than one method to solving a problem and you need to understand the range of methods that could be used so that you can help your learners select the method they find easiest to use.

CASE STUDY – JEANETTE

The following is Jeanette's recollection of how she was taught numeracy while at school.

I was never any good at numbers really. It was all a bit of a foreign language to me. I wanted to be able to do it because I knew it was important and I needed it to get on, but it meant nothing to me. A lot of rules about things I didn't understand and wasn't interested in. I couldn't see the point of it. I remember one lesson, we were meant to be doing subtraction. I could do adding up and some take away sums, but I struggled when you were meant to be taking a bigger number away from a smaller number. I couldn't see how that worked. So we were being shown this way where 'you take one from the top and put it on the door stop and you had to make sure you paid one back'. I didn't have a clue what the teacher was talking about. So I just sat at the back and looked out the window. I must have looked like I was day-dreaming because Mr Jones called me out to the front of the class and said if he was so boring, maybe I should explain how it was done. I didn't have a clue. I just wanted the ground to open up and swallow me. I still have problems with take away sums and it takes me ages to do them the only way I know how by writing out lots of little pencil marks.

REFLECTIVE TASK

What is Jeanette's informal method of solving subtraction problems? What are the problems with Jeanette using this method? What is the method of subtraction that her teacher tried to show her? What might have been Jeanette's barriers to understanding this method? What alternative method of subtraction could Jeanette be shown? What type of apparatus might be useful in helping Jeanette develop her understanding of subtraction? What is the likely impact of this event on Jeanette's confidence? What number skills does Jeanette already have?

A SUMMARY OF KEY POINTS

This chapter has examined the different barriers that can impede a learner's development of numeracy skills and appropriate ways to offer support. These have included:

> **the impact of interpersonal relationships with tutors and peers;**

> **learner attitude towards numeracy;**

> **issues associated with arithmetical language;**

> **numeracy demands of vocational and academic programmes;**

> **institutional factors influencing the development of number skills;**

> **the impact of how numeracy is taught on learning.**

Many learners struggle with numeracy and tutors can assist learners in overcoming these difficulties by providing a positive environment which supports development. Tutors need to be vigilant in addressing any personal issues they may have regarding their own numeracy skills and need to ensure they are adequately prepared to support their learners.

Learning review audit

Topic	I feel confident in doing this	This is an area I will need to develop
I can identify different personal learning barriers that impact on number skill development		
I understand the ways in which institutional factors support or hinder the development of learners' numeracy skills		
I am aware of the diagnostic testing procedures that are used in my organisation		
I know what my personal attitudes towards number are		
I understand what the numeracy requirements of my course are		

REFERENCES   REFERENCES   REFERENCES   REFERENCES   REFERENCES

Black, P and Wiliam, D (2001) *Inside the black box – raising standards through classroom assessment.* Available at http://ngfl.northumberland.gov.uk/keystage3ictstrategy/assessment/blackbox.pdf

Chanda, N, Griffiths G and Stone R (2007) *Integrating formative and diagnostic assessment techniques into teachers' routine practice in adult numeracy.* London: NRDC Publications.

Henderson, A (1998) *Maths for the dyslexic – a practical guide.* London: David Fulton.

McLaughlin, GH (1969) SMOG, simple measure of goobledegook available at www.harrymclaughlin.com/SMOG.htm

Nardi, E and Steward, S (2003) Is mathematics T.I.R.E.D.? A profile of quiet disaffection in the secondary mathematics classroom. *British Educational Research Journal,* 29: 345–67.

Newmarch, B and Part, T (2007) *Number.* London: NRDC Publications.

Rowland, T (2001) The sum of a good maths teacher. *Times Educational Supplement*, 2 February.

Swain, J and Swan, M (2007) *Thinking through mathematics research project.* London: NRDC Publications.

FURTHER READING   FURTHER READING   FURTHER READING   FURTHER READING

Aplin, R (1998) *Assisting numeracy – a handbook for classroom assistants.* London: Beam Education.

BBC (2000) *Count me in.* London: BBC Learning Support.

DfES (2001) *Adult numeracy core curriculum.* London: DfES Publications.

Fox, G and Halliwell, M (2001) *Supporting literacy and numeracy: a guide for teaching assistants.* London: David Fulton.

Wright, R et al (2006) *Early numeracy – assessment for teaching and intervention.* London: Paul Chapman Publishing.

Websites

www.literacytrust.org.uk/campaign/SMOG.html   National Literacy Trust

www.bksb.co.uk   Numeracy assessment for colleges

www.toolslibrary.co.uk/tools.htm   Numeracy assessment for the workplace

www.hoddertests.co.uk/MaLT/default.htm   Numeracy assessment for schools

www.qia.org.uk/pursuingexcellence/aims/leitch.html   Quality Improvement Agency

www.move-on.org.uk/index.asp   Move-On

4
Principal disabilities and learning difficulties relating to numeracy

By the end of this chapter you will be able to:

- name a range of disabilities and/or learning difficulties which impact on number skills development;
- identify how these different learning disabilities and difficulties affect learning numeracy skills;
- identify best practice when working with learners with disabilities and learning difficulties;
- identify a range of strategies and approaches which would support learners with disabilities and learning difficulties in the development of number skills.

Links to minimum core numeracy

This chapter relates to the following minimum core requirements.

A1   Awareness of strategies that learners can use to overcome numeracy difficulties

          Awareness of resources, specialist equipment, teaching strategies and referral procedures which could help learners overcome their numeracy difficulties

A2   Begin to address the needs of learners with learning difficulties and disabilities and seek expert advice for specific learning needs

Links to Professional Standards

AK 3.1   Issues of equality, diversity and inclusion

AP 3.1   Apply principles to evaluate and develop own practice in promoting equality and inclusive learning and engaging with diversity

BP 2.4   Apply flexible and varied delivery methods as appropriate to teaching and learning practice

BK 5.2   Ways to ensure that resources used are inclusive, promote equality and support diversity

FP 2.1   Provide effective learning support, within the boundaries of the teaching role

Links to Certificate in Teaching in the Lifelong Learning Sector (CTLLS)

Unit 2   Planning and enabling learning – how to plan for inclusive learning; how to use teaching and learning strategies and resources inclusively to meet curriculum requirements

Links to Diploma in Teaching in the Lifelong Learning Sector (DTLLS)

Unit 2   Planning and enabling learning – how to plan for inclusive learning; how to use teaching and learning strategies and resources inclusively to meet curriculum requirements

Unit 3   Enabling learning and assessment – how to apply minimum core specifications in own specialist area

Unit 4   Theories and principles for planning and enabling learning – theories and principles of learning and communication in planning and enabling inclusive practice; how to apply minimum core specifications in own specialist area

Learners with disabilities and learning difficulties: a teaching context

The minimum core requires that *teachers have an awareness of the categories in 'Access for All' and their implications for learning numeracy* (LLUK, 2007, p28). This chapter addresses that requirement and provides guidance on how teachers can work with learners with disabilities and learning difficulties to ensure they can access the curriculum and enjoy a positive learning experience.

Statistics indicate that in the UK:

- 8 million people have some form of hearing loss;
- 1,670, 000 people have a visual impairment;
- 1 in 5 people will have mental health difficulties at some stage in their life;
- 10 percent of the adult population have dyslexia;
- several million adults have physical disabilities;
- 1.2 million adults have learning difficulties.

(DfEE, 2000)

Following John Tomlinson's 1996 Report on inclusive education and the DDA (first introduced in 1995 and subsequently revised several times), learners with the disabilities and learning difficulties identified earlier are now engaging in mainstream further education, and public sector education providers are obliged to make adequate provision for this group. As a result of this legislation it is now far more likely you will encounter and need to accommodate learners with additional needs in your teaching. Although these learners share many issues in common with learners who do not have a disability or learning need, they also have different and discrete requirements that need to be met.

Learners with disabilities and learning difficulties are not just starting to learn, but may not have been successful (DfES, 2002a, p7) in their previous learning. Even though learners may be at the beginning of developing their skills it is important to use approaches and materials suitable for adult learners, rather than resources targeted at children. Provided learners are able to gain appropriate support, learners with disabilities and learning difficulties will be able to participate and achieve in mainstream education. Your role as a tutor is to ensure that learners can access the support they need and to manage your delivery of the curriculum and resources so that they are included.

This chapter describes a number of named disabilities and learning difficulties and their impact on numeracy skills. In your role as a tutor it is critical that you do not assume that learners with the same conditions will necessarily have the same needs. This chapter provides useful general guidance for working with learners with disabilities and learning difficulties. However, you will need to work with learners to determine their specific, individual needs so that appropriate resources and support can be provided.

REFLECTIVE TASK

Think about the different groups of learners you are currently teaching. How many learners in your groups have disabilities and/or learning difficulties? If you have been teaching for some time consider how many learners with additional learning needs you encountered when you began teaching. What changes have you noticed over the passage of time? What do you believe the current attitude is in your workplace towards teaching learners with disabilities and learning difficulties? Is this attitude consistent with the institution's public position on working with these learners?

Guidance on working with learners with disabilities and/or learning difficulties

If you are relatively new to teaching you may be unfamiliar with working with learners with disabilities or learning difficulties. You may feel that you are not adequately trained or have sufficient expertise to work effectively with this group. Whatever your own personal feelings may be, the stipulations of the DDA require that all public sector education providers make adequate provision and reasonable adjustments to cater for the needs of this group. In your role as a tutor you do not have the opportunity to specify which learners you are prepared to teach, and if a student with a disability or learning difficulty is allocated to one of your teaching groups, you will be obliged to teach and make provisions for them. While this might initially appear a daunting prospect if you are not accustomed to working with learners with these needs, you should remember that teaching methods which benefit learners with disabilities and learning difficulties *will help all learners* (DfES, 2002a, p9), and represent a model of best practice in teaching.

General principles of working with learners with disabilities and/or learning difficulties

When working with adult learners with disabilities and learning difficulties it is important to remember that this is not a homogenous group. Although there may be some commonalities of need if learners share a particular condition, you will also encounter learners with similar conditions and very different support needs. The variation could be as great as one learner needing specialist one-to-one support, while another learner may only need minor modifications to the curriculum before they can participate. Equally you may encounter an individual learner who requires intensive support in one curriculum area while displaying a high degree of autonomy in all other curriculum areas. Such 'spiky' learning profiles are just as prevalent for learners with disabilities and learning difficulties as they are for learners without identified conditions.

The following are useful general principles to remember.

- Ensure that you use appropriate terminology. As terminology is constantly changing to reflect society's views and values, it is your responsibility as a tutor to model best practice and to demonstrate your support for inclusion. Make sure that you are aware of current acceptable terms to describe learners with disabilities and learning difficulties and use these terms. If you are uncertain on the appropriate term to use, seek clarification from the learner, although you will need to exercise caution if requested to use youth or street slang.
- Be aware each learner you teach is an individual. When working with learners with disabilities and learning difficulties remember they have the best understanding of the implications of their own condition and what works for them. Have the confidence to make use of this expertise and be willing to seek guidance from the learners themselves.
- Work to provide a positive and supportive learning environment which values all learners and promotes achievement. Encourage group responsibility where all learners work cooperatively to develop each other's abilities. Support learning through inspiring teaching methods and by using engaging, age-appropriate learning materials.
- Develop a 'critical eye' and take note of successful (and unsuccessful) teaching approaches. Seek to maximise opportunities to include successful strategies and to minimise or remove unsuccessful strategies. Be willing to take risks and try new and innovative approaches to support learning. Work with your learners to enable them to guide you on the most appropriate ways forward.

- Make maximum use of new and assistive technology. There is now a wealth of free material available on the internet that can assist learners with a variety of numerical concepts including the four rules of number, measurement and currency. Be aware, however that computer-aided learning is not suited to all learners, and some older learners may not have developed the skills to enable them to access this technology.
- Learners with disabilities and learning difficulties will benefit from the opportunity to complete regular practice and revision. This is particularly important if the learner has a degenerative condition and they will need support to help them maintain their existing skills level.
- Arrange for a comprehensive assessment of needs to be completed through appropriate diagnostic assessment procedures which identify the learner's existing levels of knowledge and understanding. Once a full picture of needs is known, you will be more able to provide relevant support and it is more likely that the support provided will be successful.

There are many national organisations that can help in supporting learners with additional learning needs including your own professional teaching association. Some of these are suggested at the end of this chapter. However, such national networks may lack an awareness of the specific nature of your working environment and the needs of your learners. For this reason, it is also helpful to work with local support networks. The most useful of these is likely to be your own institution's internal student support services. Many education providers now have dedicated student support teams, trained in assisting learners with particular learning needs. They will be able to work closely with you and can help you in producing resources and developing strategies to meet the needs of your learners.

REFLECTIVE TASK

How many of the points raised in the general principles above do you already achieve within your own practice? If you are not currently applying these principles ask yourself 'why not?' How could you change your working practice so you could incorporate these principles? What staff development issues (if any) does this raise for you?

PRACTICAL TASK PRACTICAL TASK PRACTICAL TASK PRACTICAL TASK PRACTICAL TASK

Carry out a review of your teaching groups and identify the groups where there are learners with disabilities and/or learning difficulties. Identify the range of presenting conditions of these learners. Now itemise the types of support provided to these learners. Is this support provided by an internal support team, externally by outside agencies or do you personally provide the support needed? What additional adaptations could you make to your teaching to further enhance the learning experience of these learners?

Working with adults with identified conditions

The following guidance relates to the categories identified in *Access for All* and summarises how learning may be affected by different disabilities. For each named condition background information relating to the disability or learning difficulty is provided followed by strategies and resources to support learners. The nature of the guidance is, to a degree, general and you will need to apply this guidance so that it reflects the individual needs of your learners and the particular nature of your working environment. Remember that a learner's *approach to learning will vary in the contexts of different tasks and activities* (Beveridge, 1999, p81) and it is unlikely any one particular strategy will be suitable for all situations or all learners.

Learners who are hearing impaired

Background information

Hearing loss falls into two categories

- *Conductive deafness, where sound may not pass through either the outer or middle ear*
- *Sensorineural deafness, where the cause of deafness is located in the cochlea or the auditory nerve*

(DfES, 2001, p2)

Both forms of deafness identified can vary in degree and most adults can expect to experience some measure of hearing loss as a natural feature of aging. Depending on the learner's age and developmental learning stage when hearing loss occurred, learners may not have had the opportunity to develop mathematical language or understanding of mathematical concepts. Learners with hearing loss may not have had the same incidental number learning experiences that occur in everyday exchanges as their peers. For example they may have been excluded from conversations such as 'if there is a 3 percent increase in mortgage rates how will this affect monthly repayments?'

Numeracy has its own dedicated language and learners with hearing impairment may need to be taught this separately. Further complications are caused because it is possible to formulate the same numerical problem using different language. For example 15 divided by 5, and 5 into 15 are mathematical equivalents which might create directional or sequencing problems for learners. This could cause confusion and it might be more useful to agree what terms will be used and apply these consistently. This is particularly important if learners have more than one tutor.

Strategies and resources to support learners

Learners with hearing impairment may communicate in a variety of different ways. Some learners may use British Sign Language (BSL), others will use sign-supported English, while still others will use lip-reading or a combination of these methods. As a tutor you need to check which is the learner's preferred communication medium and aim to use this. When talking to a deaf or partially hearing learner, make sure you face them and position yourself so that your face is clearly lit. In this way the learner will be able to see the patterns your lips are making. Reduce glare in the room by using curtains or blinds. Help learners to participate in whole-class activities by using a horseshoe seating arrangement. This will help learners to easily see their peers' faces as they are speaking. When talking record key words on the board to provide visual reinforcement of important points. Reducing background noise will be helpful for all learners with hearing impairment.

Some learners communicate with the assistance of intermediaries such as a communication support worker (CSW), interpreters or signers. These are trained staff that use BSL and act as mediators between the teacher and the learner. If you have these staff in your class you should involve them in the teaching process by briefing them about the lesson, supplying them with learning materials in advance and agreeing the best strategies to support the learner. However, you need to remember that the intermediaries' role is to support the learning process and not to take primary responsibility for teaching.

If learners use BSL remember that there are regional as well as contextual variations in signs. For example a 'long' time and a 'long' distance although both numerically meaning 'greater' would be signed in different ways. Some more complex language may not have a current standardised sign equivalent. In these circumstances you may need to work with the learner to create an agreed sign for this.

Many learners who are deaf or partially hearing

> *learn best using visual reinforcement. Learning materials that include pictures, video, diagrams, and charts are likely to be easier to use than text passages. Visits outside the classroom are likely to be a successful method, as will hands-on learning*

(DfES, 2003, p293)

To support the development of mathematical language it may be useful to display wall-charts linking words for common operations to their respective symbols. An example of this sort of diagrammatic representation is shown in Figure 4.1.

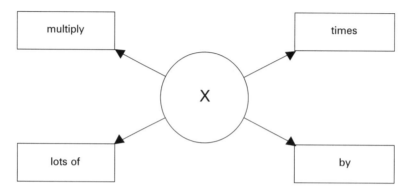

Figure 4.1 Multiplication synonyms

Practical activities related to the learners' experience and interests, rather than theoretical verbal instruction, are a good way to introduce new numerical language and concepts. For example, learners may be more interested in percentages if they understand how much money they could save in the 'everything reduced by 20 per cent' sale at the music store.

When using written materials use clear, accessible handouts with lists or bulleted points. Ensure you allow reading time for deaf learners as they cannot participate in the session until they have read the information provided and they are then able to watch you or the CSW. Because of the time lag created by communicating through an intermediary learners will need to be given time to process information before beginning calculations. Where possible aim to use source materials from deaf culture. Learners in your class who are hearing impaired should be able to assist you with this.

PRACTICAL TASK PRACTICAL TASK PRACTICAL TASK PRACTICAL TASK PRACTICAL TASK

Arrange to meet with a CSW or other language intermediary based in your college or training organisation. What is the procedure for requesting their support? What useful strategies/guidance were they able to suggest to you when working with hearing impaired learners?

Visually impaired learners

Background information

Within the context of the lifelong learning sector, a learner would be described as blind, partially sighted or visually impaired if their vision could not be corrected to normal vision by wearing contact lenses or glasses. Within a teaching context, working with learners who are visually impaired raises issues for using any printed material or working from the board. A further number-related concern for learners with sight impairments is accessing tables, charts, pictures, diagrams and graphs. As much teaching is reliant on using printed resources or centred on board work, this necessitates reconsidering how information can be most effectively delivered. Learners with sight impairments may find it difficult to think in concepts and these need to be introduced in a practical way before progressing on to abstract representation.

Strategies and resources to support learners

Because teaching using the board as a central resource can create problems for learners with visual impairments, it may be better to use small group strategies and allocate resources to each group. Rather than writing onto the board, prepare a Powerpoint presentation and provide learners with sight impairment with a copy of the presentation in advance. If you decide board work is necessary ensure you achieve maximum contrast by using black or blue pens. Different sight conditions require different lighting levels and you need to enquire what is most suitable for your learners. Generally, however, well-lit rooms and the absence of glare are helpful for most visually impaired learners. Support your delivery of visual demonstrations with further verbal explanation to reinforce understanding.

When using printed resources ensure there is good contrast. Black printed on white or yellow paper, or white printed on black is helpful. Aim to use resources produced on matt backgrounds as glossy paper can cause glare. When preparing your own handouts select a clear *sans serif* font and check with the learner that you have used an appropriate text size. Arial and comic sans in point 16 bold are particularly useful fonts. Some visually impaired learners may need written material complemented by audio tapes.

Some learners with sight impairment may have struggled to develop a concept of number or number operations such as addition, subtraction, multiplication and division. They may lack an understanding of 'five-ness' or 'eight-ness'. If you try to proceed straight to completing numeric operations such as 5×8, without providing practical exercises, they may not be able to follow. For these learners, it is important to develop their understanding through concrete experience. Dominoes, Unifix cubes and Cuisenaire rods are useful here. Learners can initially be provided with five piles of eight cubes and then asked to count how many cubes they have altogether. Learners can then progress to selecting the appropriate number of cubes themselves to complete this operation. Once learners have been able to develop their understanding of number through practical experience they should be able to complete number operations without aids.

For learners at the beginning of developing their number skills it is useful to have plastic representations of integers which learners can then match to the corresponding number of Unifix cubes to help them understand the value of the different numerals. Being able to hold and feel the integers helps to reinforce meaning. Other useful resources include large display and talking calculators. If learners have their own laptop, screen settings can be changed to enlarge the calculator function. Alternatively, learners can link their personal computer to a magnification or speech output device.

Learners can be supported in producing graphs and charts by using pre-printed graph paper with thick black lines. Alternatively you can create your own squared paper and photocopy multiple sheets. This is a useful aid when completing columnar addition or subtraction as it ensures that learners allocate numerals to the correct place value. Difficulties in reading and using scales on rulers and protractors can be aided by using tactile aids which have raised textured number divisions. When working with weights learners may find it easier to use talking scales. Help learners to develop their understanding of space and shape by providing plastic shapes of common polygons. These can also have different textures to further aid learning. Learners can make their own 2D representations of common shapes by using elastic bands and geoboards. When describing 3D shapes such as cuboids, spheres and cylinders, provide solid examples before asking learners to represent these in 2D form.

REFLECTIVE TASK

How accessible is your current teaching approach for learners with sight impairment? How accessible is the physical environment? Could learners with visual impairment easily move around the classes where you teach? How easy would it be for a visually impaired learner to use your resources? How reliant are you on central board work?

Learners with mental health difficulties

Background information

It is not easy to define 'mental health difficulties' because the term encompasses a diversity of feelings, thoughts, behaviours and experiences. However, one way of looking at it is to consider mental health along a continuum from serious mental ill-health through to positive mental well-being. Most of us move back and forth along this continuum throughout our lives.

(DfES, 2003, p24)

Mental health difficulties may be long or short term. Some people will experience repeated episodes of concern, while others make a full and complete recovery. Negative public attitudes towards mental health difficulties have created a situation where this group has become stigmatised or *regarded as dangerous and if not 'bad', then 'mad' or 'sad'* (DfES, 2003, p29). People with mental health difficulties experience a variety of concerns relating to education, including being unable to learn certain skills or needing to relearn skills they were previously competent in. They may lack confidence and, assuming failure, become withdrawn. Medication or sleep disturbance can cause low energy levels and they may find it difficult to concentrate for protracted periods of time. They can appear confused. Mood changes and irritability may affect their learning, so that learners find it difficult to engage or even to attend sessions. They may have gaps in their knowledge and understanding arising from earlier absences from education. Learners may not have an awareness of accepted behaviour in group situations and can display unsuitable behaviours or share sensitive information inappropriately. While it can be useful for tutors to know something of learners' lives outside of college, it is important to maintain appropriate professional boundaries.

Strategies and resources to support learners

Learners with mental health difficulties will need a supportive environment which is safe. However, it is important that college should not become like home, as this would not assist participation in mainstream education. You should create a welcoming atmosphere in which learners can relax and feel comfortable but which is primarily focused on learning. For this reason clear ground rules will need to be established so that learners know what is expected within a learning environment and inappropriate behaviours are minimised. Aim to give control back to learners by allowing them to make real choices about their learning and empower them by allowing them to complete their work independently.

Many learners experience anxiety when completing number tasks. However, this anxiety can be intensified and greater for those learners with mental health difficulties. For this reason it is important to introduce number work in a staged fashion. Keep exposure to concepts to a manageable level and do not overburden learners with too many new ideas at once. If learners should start to display signs of anxiety help them to manage their stress by changing activity, taking 'time out' or doing simple relaxation exercises. Learners may become particularly anxious if there is a change in normal routines, for example if the usual tutor is absent through in-service training. Learners can be helped through this situation by inform-ing them of the changes in advance and, if absolutely necessary, giving them the opportunity to miss the session. This final strategy should, however, only be used as an unavoidable last option. Alternatively a familiar face, such as a support worker, could attend the session with the learner to provide continuity. Group exercises and games which are often used to teach numerical ideas can be challenging to learners with mental health concerns as they involve working with other learners. If you choose to use group strategies remember to incorporate space for individual activity in these sessions.

CASE STUDY – DAVID

David, who has mental health difficulties, attends your basic skills numeracy class. This is a mainstream provision and David is the only learner in the group who has been identified as having mental health concerns. Initially David came to the session with a support worker but now attends independently. David has his own individual learning plan (ILP) and has been completing work on multiplication. You introduced this topic by asking David to use Unifix cubes to work out simple multiplication problems and at the end of your last session you showed David a method to complete this calculation without using practical aids. At the start of the following session David spent at least 20 minutes pacing up and down outside of the class and refused to come into the session. When asked why he would not join the group, he replied, 'the way maths is taught at college is wrong, and that's not how they did times sums at school'.

REFLECTIVE TASK

What issues does David's behaviour raise? What has happened to increase David's anxiety? What actions should the class tutor now take? What issues does this raise for the teaching strategies selected? What steps will need to be taken to reintegrate David into the class? How can David be reassured of the tutor's ability to teach numeracy? What is the role of the college's support services in this situation? What is the role of David's peers in this situation?

Learners with dyslexia

Dyslexia is a literacy and language condition associated with *difficulty in reading, spelling and written language* (DfES, 2003, p210). There is a second condition, dyscalculia, which is associated with number difficulties. Although dyscalculia is not described in *Access for All*, information about this condition is provided within this chapter.

Background information

Because education in the UK is built around written and verbal communication, learners with dyslexia are disadvantaged in accessing the curriculum. So that learners can make progress with their work, appropriate support needs to be provided. Learners with dyslexia may experience difficulties in some or all the following areas.

- Phonological awareness – learners experience difficulties with letter sounds, letter blends, vowels and word segmentation.
- Auditory discrimination – learners have problems with recognising or hearing the difference between similar sounds like p, b and v.
- Sequencing – learners with dyslexia may find it hard to remember the correct sequence of letters for words.
- Organisational skills – learners may find it difficult to produce their own plans to complete multi-stage tasks or written work.

Learners with dyslexia may also experience difficulty with number work which has its own symbolic language, although there is no proven link between dyslexia and dyscalculia. Dyslexic learners may also experience difficulty with specific numerical language, memorising number, confusing mathematical symbols such as $\div$ and $\times$, transposing number information or columnar operations due to poor visual tracking.

Strategies and resources to support learners

Dyslexic learners may find it more supportive to work in smaller groups where they can receive greater support. White backgrounds for printed materials are usually unsuitable for learners with dyslexia and pastel coloured paper will be more useful. When producing worksheets for learners, check which background colour is most suitable for them. Alternatively learners could be provided with coloured acetate overlays to work with. This may be more helpful as learners can use these with any printed material. If producing a PowerPoint presentation, remember that you too need to change the background colour of your slides. Larger font sizes can assist with visual tracking.

Because of the effort that it takes for a learner with dyslexia to concentrate, it is useful to break up activities into smaller sections and to alternate written tasks with verbal activities. Provide detailed explanations of errors made so that the learner is aware of both *what* their mistake is and *how* the error occurred. For columnar operations use squared paper to indicate the different place values of number, or differentiate between place value by using coloured highlighters.

Use diagrams or flowcharts to help learners understand the sequence of particular mathematical operations. For example the calculation $x = \frac{20 \times 5}{15} + \frac{44 \times 3}{12}$ would be more helpfully described as:

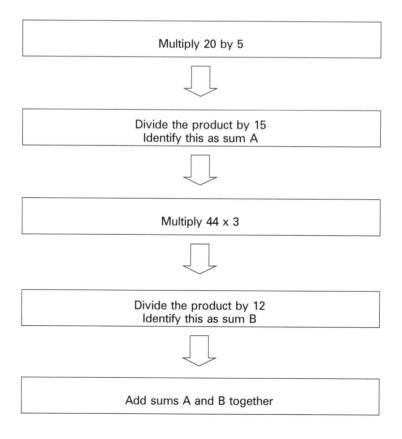

Multiply 20 by 5

Divide the product by 15
Identify this as sum A

Multiply 44 x 3

Divide the product by 12
Identify this as sum B

Add sums A and B together

For learners beginning number work it may be useful to use resources such as Unifix and other resources described in strategies for visually impaired learners.

PRACTICAL TASK PRACTICAL TASK **PRACTICAL TASK** PRACTICAL TASK **PRACTICAL TASK**

Identify some common numerical operations you complete with your groups. Prepare flowcharts you could use with learners to indicate how these operations should be completed.

Learners with dyscalculia

Background information

Dyscalculia is a *dysfunction in the reception, comprehension, or production of quantitative and spatial information* (Sharma, 2003, skillswise). Dyscalculia is the arithmetic equivalent of dyslexia, and is sometimes referred to as 'number blindness'. Dyscalculia will mean that a person experiences significant difficulties in understanding number, the effect of number operations and spatial information. Consequently, individuals will have serious difficulties in performing even the most basic number operations. Unfortunately, there is *no formal diagnostic test specifically for dyscalculia* although *a useful dyscalculia screener for teachers* (British Dyslexia Association, 2007) has been developed by Professor Brian Butterworth and is available from NFER-Nelson. Because of lack of awareness about the condition many learners with dyscalculia remain undiagnosed. This situation is further complicated as many learners experience difficulty when working with number and it is not easy to distinguish what might be considered to be a 'normal' level of anxiety and error from genuine dyscalculia.

Strategies and resources to support learners

Advice on strategies to support dyscalculic learners has been hampered because *there has been much less research on dyscalculia than on dyslexia, and it is a much less widely recognised type of learning disability* (Butterworth and Yeo, 2004, p1). To carry out mathematical operations learners need to understand *number, place value, fractions, integers, spatial sense and variability* (Sharma, 2003, skillswise). All of these are potential areas of difficulty for the dyscalculic learner and screening will need to be completed to determine which specific area the learner is experiencing difficulty in. Learners will then need to be taken back to that point and their understanding built up in a systematic fashion. Learners will need specialist intervention to help them progress, although all tutors can support the process by:

- providing opportunities for repetition and practice of arithmetic facts;
- supporting learners in forming problems to a given concept;
- giving learners opportunities to break down a task into its constituent parts and organising these into a whole sequence to solve a given problem;
- questioning learners in a structured way to help them build up the correct sequence to solve a numerical problem.

Learners with physical disabilities

Background information

Our views of *disability are often closely tied up with notions of mobility* but this notion can be problematic as it can *mask the wide variety of individual difference which exists within that group* (Glen, 1992, p159). Physical disability describes a wide range of conditions which may be *temporary or permanent, fluctuating, stable or degenerative and may affect parts of the body or the whole of it* (DfES, 2002a, p33) and can be *mildly, moderately or severely disabling* (Glen, 1992, p159). Whatever the causes and level of disability, learners are entitled to *a good education that enables them to achieve their full potential* (DfES, 2004, p8).

An initial concern for learners with physical disabilities is gaining access to the building where learning occurs and being able to move safely around the building. This is particularly an issue with older premises although from September 2005 organisations have been *required to make adjustments to physical features of premises where these put disabled people or learners at a substantial disadvantage* (DfES, 2003, p355). Other disabilities learners may have include:

- poor motor control creating difficulties in writing;
- speech difficulties which hinder verbal communication; or
- perceptual difficulties which influence understanding of ideas and concepts.

Strategies and resources to support learners

Matching your teaching style to a learner's preferred learning style *is essential for learners with learning difficulties and disabilities, who may be able to only use some styles of learning* (DfES, 2002a, p44). Learning should closely reflect learners' skills and interests and you may need to produce a personalised learning plan to achieve this. For example a learner may have a particular interest in a local sports team or a particular type of music. Numeracy work could be developed on revenues of ticket sales, percentage increase in ticket prices, the total wage bill for the team or travel times to away games. Alternatively, a programme of work could be constructed on the number of downloads, tour dates and the average crowd capacity at venues. There is often considerable overlap between this group of learners and other learners with disabilities. Consequently, strategies suggested elsewhere in this chapter are also likely to be helpful when working with this group.

Some learners with physical disabilities may require specialised equipment to help them complete their work. There is a variety of assistive technology available to support learners including:

- copy holders to support learners' documents;
- pens and pencils with different grips and sizes;
- wrist and arm rests;
- frames to hold documents steady and enable learners to follow words and lines of text;
- separate keyboards with different designs;
- key-guards and overlays;
- handheld thesaurus and talking dictionaries;
- predictive word processing packages.

(DfES, 2003, pp376–7)

It is important to remember that the disability may affect the speed at which a learner can complete a task and sufficient time needs to be provided for learners to complete their work. If it is possible to reduce the output required by the learner without compromising learning objectives, this should be explored. This may involve providing partially completed tasks where learners are only required to complete essential information or gapped worksheets where learners need only supply short answers.

Learners with learning difficulties

Background information

The term *learning difficulties* covers a broad spectrum of needs from very mild to profound and multiple difficulties, and describes cognitive, sensory, emotional, language and health conditions which may affect a learner's development of skills, knowledge and understanding within an educational context. *Four degrees of learning difficulty* are recognised: *mild, moderate, specific and severe* (Gulliford, 1992, p42). The learning needs of this group are very diverse and the type of support required by the learner will vary according to the nature and level of learning difficulty.

Learners with learning difficulties may have had damaging previous learning experiences and, fearful of future failure, may display a lack confidence in their abilities. Tutors need to work with learners to develop learning programmes which provide them with stimulating educational challenges that reflect their abilities and interests.

Strategies and resources to support learners

To help promote achievement for this group teaching should be *structured, sequential (and) cumulative* (Gulliford, 1992, p50). Initially tutors will need to establish a climate for learning by setting realistic but achievable targets for learners. Tutors should help learners to direct their own learning by encouraging them to identify goals and by providing them with choices within the overall framework of their programme. Learners are more likely to show interest in learning if they can see the relevance of an activity or it is embedded in their own life experience. As learners attempt or complete tasks, you will need to provide positive feedback which recognises achievement or progress towards goals. This can then be used as a basis to plan future learning.

Learners with learning difficulties will need a personalised learning programme delivered through appropriate teaching strategies and supported with relevant resources. Learners in this group share much in common with other learners described in this chapter and suggestions provided earlier are also applicable to these learners.

PRACTICAL TASK PRACTICAL TASK **PRACTICAL TASK** PRACTICAL TASK **PRACTICAL TASK**

Think about the learners you teach with learning difficulties. What are their particular strengths? How do you help learners to build on these strengths? What barriers do these learners experience? What issues does this raise for their studies with you? How could you develop your teaching strategies to provide greater opportunities for learners with learning difficulties?

Learners with autistic spectrum disorders

Background information

Autistic spectrum disorders (ASD, also known as autistic spectrum conditions, ASC) describes a range of conditions which vary in degree, including classic autism, Asperger's syndrome and pathological demand avoidance (PDA). However, all conditions are linked by concerns in three areas, often referred to as the 'triad of impairments'. These areas, shown in Figure 4.2, are interlinked and interact with and affect each other.

Although diagnosis usually takes place by the time a person is five years old, it may not occur until adulthood. This situation is compounded by the absence of a *conclusive diagnostic test and it is quite common for professionals to disagree over the diagnosis* (DfES, 2002b, p9). The condition is more common in males than females, with approximately four times as many men being diagnosed with ASD. There is no known single cause for the condition, though it is now generally accepted to result from *a strong genetic component (and) environmental factors* (DfES, 2002b, p12). There is no cure for ASD and learners will continue to experience the features of ASD throughout their lives.

Learners with ASD can be very literal thinkers and may not understand how meaning changes according to context. They may have difficulty in understanding the assumed

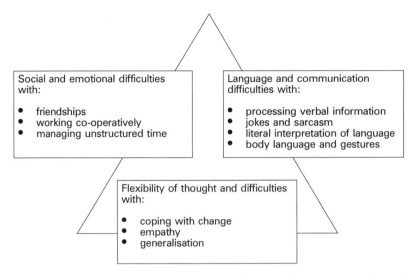

Source: Surrey County Council (2004, p4)

Figure 4.2 The triad of impairments

rules of social engagement and appear awkward in group situations, sometimes hovering on the fringes lacking the necessary skills to interact with others. Learners will need to be taught the skills needed for successful social interaction. Changes to established patterns can be challenging or threatening to learners with ASD, who will need guidance on how to generalise so they can apply previous learning to new situations.

Strategies and resources to support learners

Security is very important to learners with ASD. Learners will need time to become familiar with their new tutors, and pre-course visits may be necessary to introduce learners to tutors before the programme begins. Unstructured times including breaks and lunchtimes can be difficult for learners with ASD, and can cause learners to become distracted from taught sessions, as they worry about what will happen during unsupervised time. Tutors can assist here by identifying 'safe zones' for learners such as the ICT suite or the library. If unstructured time becomes problematic, a named person will need to be identified that students can contact during these periods. Establishing routines which learners are comfortable with will help to support learning. Learners need to be given clear, unambiguous instructions so that they know exactly what is expected of them. The conversational opening of 'shall we do some number work today?', may appear as a question to the learner with ASD, who may not wish to do numeracy at all.

Learners with ASD can demonstrate good computational skills, being able to work out complex numerical problems, but will be unable to apply their skills to real-life situations. Try to find ways of embedding problems into concrete examples which learners can relate to – for example large numbers could be considered in terms of total sums repayable on a mortgage, or the size of the institution's teaching budget. Learners will be more able to engage in a task if they can see the purpose and the function of the activity.

Some skills like estimation, approximation, choosing which data to collect for a project and mathematical reasoning are likely to be areas of difficulty for learners with ASD as they involve thinking imaginatively and creating solutions rather than applying formulas. Learners will need to be supported by being given concrete examples and templates which they can apply in these situations. Many students with ASD relate well to visual learning strategies and the suggestions in the section on working with learners with hearing impairment may be useful.

Case Study – Michael

Michael has ASD. In his first year at college he was in a dedicated group for learners with ASD. At the start of his second year he was integrated into your mainstream BTEC level 2 computing class. Michael has one friend, Paul, who he always sits next to. Michael is a very quiet person and only speaks to you when you ask him a direct question. He does not actively participate in whole-class activities and either works independently or with his single friend. He has good computing skills and his work is usually of a high standard.

For part of the year-end assessment all learners worked in small groups and prepared a 'sales pitch' to demonstrate the cost benefits of a software package to a local business person. Michael worked with his friend and a third student, Daniel. Michael was initially unsettled by this but managed to work with the two other learners. The final presentation was carefully set up and you continually, although unobtrusively, checked Michael was coping with this situation. On the day of the presentation two groups gave their sales pitches and you then invited Michael's group to make their presentation. Daniel began the presentation and was meant to be followed by Michael. However, Michael erupted explosively, swearing at you, telling how he hated the course, could not see the point of the work and ripped up his own group's sales poster. He then turned two tables over, and stormed out, only to return almost immediately when he ripped up a second group's poster before finally leaving the college premises.

REFLECTIVE TASK

As the class tutor how would you manage this situation? What immediate actions would you/should you take? How will you support the members of Michael's group and the other class members? How would you work with the invited business person? Who does this incident need to be reported to? What are the safety issues of Michael leaving the college premises? What impact will this have on assessment for the two groups whose work was damaged? How else could you have managed this assessment activity to meet the assessment requirements of the course? If verbal presentations were a mandatory assessment component how could this presentation have been set up to reduce pressure on Michael?

A SUMMARY OF KEY POINTS

This chapter considered:

> how the culture of education has moved towards an inclusive ethos;

> the different types of disability and learning difficulties specified in *Access for All*;

> how disability and learning difficultly may impact on the development of number skills;

> how tutors can work to support learners in their development of number skills;

> assistive resources that can be used to support learners with numeracy.

Although all tutors in the lifelong learning sector are not numeracy tutors, all tutors have a professional responsibility to develop the numeracy skills of the learners they work with. This means having a clear understanding of learners' skills levels and an awareness of the different conditions which may influence number development. Learning will be more successful if learners are supported appropriately, and while this is true of all learners, it becomes vital for learners who have additional needs. Tutors will need to develop their own understanding of conditions and access to support networks, so that they can provide a positive learning experience for learners.

Learning review audit

Topic	I feel confident in doing this	This is an area I will need to develop
I can name the principal learning disabilities and difficulties that impact on number skills development		
I am aware of specialist equipment and assistive technology that would be useful to the learners I teach		
I know what internal support services are available where I work		
I can identify specialist support services that would be able to assist the learners I teach and know how to contact these agencies		
I can identify ways I could adapt my delivery to accommodate learners' learning disabilities and difficulties		

REFERENCES   REFERENCES   REFERENCES   REFERENCES   REFERENCES

Beveridge, S (1999) *Special educational needs in schools*. London: RoutledgeFalmer.

British Dyslexia Association (2007) *Dyscalculia, dyslexia and maths*. Available at www.bdadyslexia.org.uk/dyslexia.html

Butterworth, B and Yeo, D (2004) *Dyscalculia guidance*. Cheltenham: NFER-Nelson.

DfEE (2000) *Freedom to learn: basic skills for learners with learning difficulties and/or disabilities*. Nottingham: DfEE Publications.

DfES (2001) *Guidance to support pupils with hearing impairments*. Nottingham: DfES Publications.

DfES (2002a) *Access for all: guidance on making the adult literacy and numeracy core curricula accessible*. London: DfES Publications.

DfES (2002b) *Autistic spectrum disorders: good practice guidance. 1: Guidance on autistic spectrum disorders*. Nottingham: DfES Publications.

DfES (2003) *Basic skills for learners with learning difficulties or disabilities: a resource pack to support staff development*. Nottingham: DfES Publications.

DfES (2004) *Removing barriers to achievement: the Government's strategy for SEN – Executive summary*. Nottingham: DfES Publications.

Fox, G and Halliwell, M (2001) *Supporting literacy and numeracy: a guide for teaching assistants*. London: David Fulton.

Glen, I (1992) Physical Disabilites, in Gulliford, R and Upton, G (eds) *Special Educational Needs*. London: Routledge.

Gulliford, R (1992) Learning Difficulties, in Gulliford, R and Upton, G (eds) *Special Educational Needs.* London: Routledge.

LLUK (2007) *Addressing literacy, language, numeracy and ICT needs in education and training: defining the minimum core of teachers' knowledge, understanding and personal skills.* London: LLUK.

Sharma, M (2003) *Dyscalculia.* Available at www.bbc.co.uk/skillswise/tutors/expertcolumn/dyscalculia/

Surrey County Council (2004) *Breaking down barriers to learning: Practical strategies for achieving successful transition for students with autism and Asperger's syndrome.* Guildford: Surrey County Council

Tomlinson, J (1996) *Inclusive learning report of the Learning Difficulties and Disabilities Committee*. Coventry: Further Education Funding Council

FURTHER READING FURTHER READING **FURTHER READING** FURTHER READING

Anderson, V, Faraday S, Prowse S, Richards G, Swindells D (2003) *Count me in FE.* London: Learning and skills development agency

Butterworth, B (2004) *Dyscalculia guidance: helping pupils with specific learning difficulties in maths*. London: David Fulton.

DfES (2004) *Children with autism: strategies for accessing the curriculum.* DfES Publications.

Henderson, A (1998) *Maths for the dyslexic: a practical guide.* London: David Fulton.

Websites

www.rnid.org.uk   Royal National Institute for the Deaf

www.nated.org.uk   National Association of Tertiary Education for Deaf People (NATED)

www.rnib.org.uk   Royal National Institute for the Blind

www.mentalhealth.org.uk   Mental Health Foundation

www.mind.org.uk   MIND

www.bdadyslexia.org.uk   British Dyslexia Association

www.learningdisabilities.org.uk   Foundation for People with Learning Disabilities

www.nas.org.uk   National Autistic Society

5
Numeracy and participation in public life

Thinking about number

This chapter is about the centrality of number in our lives. It is intended to help you think about all the different ways in which your learners may encounter number, and how your learners' competence with numbers will in turn influence their experiences and the outcomes of those experiences. This chapter demonstrates how success and difficulty in many social and employment situations, probably in equal measure, can be traced back to a competence, or not, in using number and different number skills.

In the first instance it is important to recognise the prevalence of number in society in general, and in particular how number features in our own lives. Number and number skills are embedded in every aspect of our social and working lives. Number is all around us, all the time, and it exerts a profound influence on how we live and how we work. From the moment we wake up, until we switch off the light to sleep, in some way we find ourselves using and, more importantly, needing to use number skills. Number skills are used when we go shopping, top up the credit on our mobile phones, pay our bills, keep score when we play games or sports or work out the quantity of materials we need when we decorate our homes. To imagine a life without number skills would be to imagine a life in which routine tasks would either become more difficult, or we would be prevented from taking part in these activities at all. Without adequate number skills we are not living but coping, reliant on 'make-do' strategies which may be enough to enable us to manage but will not be sufficient to support our full engagement with and active participation in society. Put simply, if we lack number skills, *we don't get on, we get by* (DfES, 2004).

If you have developed your number skills from an early age and are competent and confident in using number, you probably won't even think about all the different skills that you use. You will be able to work out number problems quickly, not paying attention to the multiple sequences of operations you apply or the knowledge you use. If this describes you and your experience you can describe yourself as numerate – you are able to use your number skills and knowledge in a wide variety of different settings to help you function and achieve.

Number is not a contained, marginalised skill, but is integrated into every aspect of our daily lives. Number is a central life skill.

REFLECTIVE TASK

Consider the points raised in the introductory section, and identify the number skills you regularly use in a 24-hour period. What number skills do you need to help you start the day? How are number skills used on your journey to work? If you have children or care for relatives, how do you use your number skills in working with them? How easy would it be to carry out your job if you had poorly developed or underdeveloped number skills?

PRACTICAL TASK PRACTICAL TASK PRACTICAL TASK PRACTICAL TASK PRACTICAL TASK

To provide some structure to your thoughts and to help you capture all the different number skills that you use, draw out a time line or number grid, like the one below, and itemise, according to the time you need to complete an activity or task, the number skills, knowledge of number facts or processes needed to complete the activity. An example has been provided to guide you. Try to work with a colleague or friend to identify all the ways in which you routinely use number in your daily activities. Compare and contrast your experiences and the number skills level you need to complete your daily tasks.

Time	Task	Factors to consider	Number skills involved
08:45	Buy petrol	Bit short of cash this week. Decide to only put £30 in, rather than fill up. Pay with two £20 notes	Budgeting and estimating cash flow Currency recognition Multiplication: $2 \times £20 = £40$ Receive change: subtraction

Defining numeracy

There is no agreed and universally accepted term to define and describe numeracy. Internationally, numeracy is used to describe different sets of numerical skills, processes and knowledge in different countries. This situation is also evident within the UK, where the term is continually evolving and changing as diverse groups seek to define and redefine the term to suit their own purposes. Various interest groups, including political parties, community organisations, schools and colleges, can all be seen to be using different working definitions of numeracy which, although they may share some commonalities, also differ in significant ways. Numeracy, as a term remains in a state of flux and change. To a degree, this lack of agreement reflects the fact that numeracy is a relatively modern term. Indeed the recent arrival of the word is reflected in the fact that many word-processing packages still do not recognise the word, indicating it as a spelling error and offering numeric as the correct alternative.

Numeracy first appeared in an educational context in the UK in the 1959 Crowther Report where it was presented as the mathematical equivalent to literacy. The word itself though, has a much older root, stemming from the Latin *numare*, which literally means to count or to enumerate. This in itself is a relatively simple process and only requires that objects are totalled by using a number system. It is worthwhile noting here that in history there have been various number systems (Roman numerals represent a different but familiar system), but all have served the same function – a way of determining the quantity and the position of objects within a particular environment. As a skill, the ability to count and to recognise and allocate numerals correctly can be viewed as an elementary but essential number skill. Individuals will need to understand this process and be able to use it competently before moving on to other more complicated processes. Counting is one of the initial building blocks needed to develop number skills successfully. Numeracy, however, is usually perceived as a far wider skill and has come to mean the ability to use a range of different, and sometimes complex, number skills within differing environments.

Tout (2002, p1) developed this view by stating that numeracy is primarily concerned with *the use of mathematics in real situations.* This description and distinction is significant. Although mathematics uses all the skills, knowledge and processes that are found in numeracy, it also includes many more abstract skills. Many learners in the past have found it difficult to identify the functional or practical use of such abstract mathematical concepts as trigonometry or algebra, and have viewed these skills as the preserve of 'brainy geeks'. For these learners, mathematics was seen as a pursuit for elite academics. Consequently these learners chose to reject mathematics as it held little interest for them and had no obvious purpose or meaning. This negative view of mathematics continues to this day for many learners, who still believe that mathematics is 'not for the likes of them'. Numeracy distinguishes itself from mathematics because it seeks to establish a tangible link between number skills and everyday life. Numeracy further distinguishes itself because it does not contain skills which have no practical application. Numeracy can be described as the functional, useful skills which learners need to support them in achieving daily tasks. Whereas mathematics could be viewed as an exclusive pursuit for a talented and exceptional few, numeracy aims to be down-to-earth, relevant and inclusive. Because of its practical relevance, numeracy supports individuals and groups in taking a full and active part in society and produces positive benefits for individuals and, as a result, whole communities.

Useful number skills

Whether or not a skill is useful will depend on a number of different factors. Can you identify a need for the skill? Is it relevant to your circumstances? Will it benefit you in any way? Importantly, have you been directed or instructed to gain the skill? Equally importantly, will there be a penalty of any kind if you fail to acquire the skill? All of these factors will influence your feelings and thoughts on whether or not you decide that a skill is useful or not. The usefulness of a skill is therefore contingent on the environment in which you are operating and the purpose for which you intend to use or need the skill. Within the context of being a tutor in the lifelong learning sector, number skills are important for you on an individual basis in managing budgets, projecting learner enrolment figures and calculating the achievement and retention rates of the learners you teach. Furthermore the requirements of the minimum core numeracy direct you to locate opportunities to support learners in developing their number skills through the academic or vocational subjects you teach.

Your acceptance into society and your ability to operate within society is contingent on and underpinned by your development of appropriate numeracy skills. Adults are expected to have developed their number skills from an early age, and by the time they reach adulthood should be able to use, and need to use, a wide range of different number skills. Society's acceptance of you is conditional on your developing the relevant skills needed by society.

Society does not *request* that you are numerate, but *demands* this of you. Although it is not a crime to be innumerate and no specific identified penalty will follow if you do not comply, society registers its disapproval of your poor or underdeveloped number skills by limiting the opportunities that are available to you.

Number skills in daily life: participation in and access to society

Although it is important that you have relevant and sufficiently developed number skills, it is also important that in your role as a tutor you develop an awareness of the number skills your learners may have and the situations in which they may encounter number. This could be in your capacity as a personal tutor, or could equally occur in your vocational or academic teaching role. If you are a key skills, basic skills or mathematics tutor both your own and your learners' encounters with number will be many and obvious. The following two case studies provide an opportunity to consider some of the different number skills that your learners may need or use in their daily activities, and how their personal number skills may influence events in their lives.

CASE STUDY – SOFIA

Sofia is a single, unemployed mother of two children and has recently started attending college after being rehoused in the local area. Adam is four and attends the college playgroup while his mother is in her lessons and Sam, who is five, has just started at the local primary school. Both of the children are well cared for. Sofia's motivation for attending college is to try and gain qualifications which will help her find employment once the children are both at school. On Monday Sofia was 15 minutes late for your session on globalisation. In this session it appeared to you that Sofia was becoming increasingly agitated as you tried to explain the moral case for buying equitably produced goods, even though they may be slightly more expensive than supermarket brands. At break you noticed that Sofia did not join her peers when they went for a coffee break. When the session ended, you asked Sofia if everything was OK, or if something was bothering her. To your surprise Sofia began to cry quietly, and told you that the reason she was late for the lesson was she had received a visit from a doorstop moneylender as she had fallen behind with her repayments. By the time she had explained her situation to him, she was late for her bus to college. She had taken out a £100 loan, as she was short of money and needed to buy Sam's new school uniform. Sofia was now sick with worry as the moneylender had told her he would be back at the end of the week and expected her to have the money to pay him. The moneylender knows where she lives and she is frightened of what he will do. Sofia apologises for not being more engaged with the session but there was no way she could consider buying expensive, fairly produced goods when she was having problems making ends meet and did not know how she was going to pay the moneylender back.

This is only the briefest of snapshots into one learner's life. It is unlikely you will hear disclosures like this regularly, but it is equally unlikely you will avoid either directly being involved in or hearing of a situation similar to this, during your time as a tutor. This example raises significant issues both in terms of numeracy and in terms of your responsibilities as a tutor.

1. Tutor responsibilities

It is important to note that as a tutor it is not your responsibility to try and resolve Sofia's immediate financial problems by offering to lend (or give) her £100 to pay off the moneylender, although by the time interest has been added to the debt, £100 would not be sufficient to clear the loan. However, it is part of your responsibility to have an awareness of the services or agencies that can help Sofia with these problems. Your role in this case is to direct Sofia to the appropriate agencies and support systems so that she can begin to address these problems. This could involve helping Sofia set up an appointment with the student welfare or finance officer, or it might involve referring her on to outside support agencies such as debt counsellors.

As a tutor it is your responsibility to ensure that your learners feel comfortable and are able to learn in your sessions. This means taking many different factors into account, including whether or not some subject areas could be potentially difficult or compromising for your learners. Discussing high-value goods with low-income learners or learners who are in receipt of benefit could demonstrate insensitivity to learner needs and it would be more appropriate to choose different examples to illustrate your point.

2. Sofia's number skills

By the time Sofia arrives at your session she has already used a variety of different number skills which may not be immediately apparent. She has ensured that her two children are ready for school and the college playgroup. This involved skills in using time and estimation skills to ensure that she had sufficient opportunity to complete her routine morning tasks. If she had not received an unexpected visit, Sofia would have arrived to your lesson on time. Before she even caught the bus to college, Sofia would have had to calculate the most cost-effective way to travel to college – should she buy a bus pass, or would it be better value to buy daily tickets? To catch the bus Sofia will have needed to consult the bus timetable so she can work out at what time she will arrive at college. These timetables are often written in the 24-hour clock. When she boards the bus Sofia will need to make further financial decisions. Is it better value to buy a group ticket for herself and the children, or should she buy individual tickets for all of them? In paying the bus fare, Sofia will have needed to recognise coins and notes if she has had to pay the exact fare or she may have needed to check she has been given the correct change. Whatever way Sofia decided to pay for the bus fare, she will have needed to use money-handling skills. Once she is in your lesson Sofia is again using different number skills by recognising the financial impact of buying fairly-produced goods could have on her family's shopping bills. Sofia further demonstrates an awareness of finance by staying away from the canteen at break-time and not spending money unnecessarily. As Sofia is unemployed she will be receiving a benefit payment of some kind, and as she has two children she will automatically receive child benefit which is paid to all families regardless of income level. To make sure that her children are 'well cared for' as you are told in the case study, it would appear that generally Sofia is using well-developed budgeting skills.

3. Sofia's number problems

From the information you have been provided with in the case study, it does not appear that Sofia has significant number problems. In the completion of her many and varied daily tasks she has already shown that she is able to handle money and budget, and she can use both 24-hour and standard time. However, Sofia now finds herself with a problem involving number. She took out the £100 loan as it was a quick and convenient way to access money. She was told it was not a long-term loan and it would only take her a year to clear the debt, paying £3.50 back each week. Sofia felt she could easily manage this small amount. This is the core of Sofia's number problems. If Sofia had multiplied her weekly repayments by the number of weeks in a year she would have been able to see that she would have had to pay back a total sum of £182. Sofia was being charged 82 per cent interest. High Street banks currently charge between seven and nine per cent interest, but because Sofia has a poor credit rating and because she only wished to borrow a relatively small amount, she has had to access finance from the alternative economy. Even if Sofia were to suddenly acquire funds, she would still have the same sized debt, as most doorstop lenders offer no incentive for early repayment, and although the credit agreement that Sofia signed would have stated there was an 82 per cent rate of interest, this would have been obscured in the small print. If Sofia had had a better understanding of percentages (and possibly of multiplication) she might have realised she was being charged an exploitative amount of interest and she might have tried other options. It is important to note here that doorstop money lending is a legal and regulated process. Sofia's number problems would be far worse if she had taken a loan from an unregulated loan shark. Loan sharks charge even higher rates of interest than doorstop lenders and are known to use violence and intimidation to recover debts.

Sofia's situation is not unique, outlandish or unusual. It is a situation that you are likely to encounter at some time. You will need the appropriate skills and knowledge to support learners like Sofia in a positive way to help them address these problems.

CASE STUDY – ALAN

Alan, who is in your tutor group, recently started a part-time evening job working in the warehouse section of a large supermarket. Alan lives by himself in Council accommodation and receives housing benefit which is paid directly into his rent account. He tells you how much he enjoys his new job and is particularly happy because all employees are given a staff discount card which helps to reduce his weekly shopping bills. However, Alan is worried because he has received a verbal warning as a result of being late for his shift three times in the last month. There is no problem with the quality of his work, but his employers are starting to become concerned about his lateness. When you ask Alan about the problem with his timekeeping, he explains it is because his watch is broken and he is going to buy a new one. Alan's poor timekeeping in his job is a mystery to you because he appears to have no trouble arriving on time for lessons in college. On several other occasions you have noticed Alan with large jars of loose change which he tells you he takes to the change-counting machine in the foyer of the supermarket where he works. Alan appears to have more loose change jars than you would ordinarily expect. When Alan buys his lunch or goes for a coffee break you have also noticed that he usually pays with notes. If he does pay with coins he places a handful of change on the counter and asks the assistant to 'take what they need'. He does not seem to count the change, but stuffs this in his pocket while he puts any notes away carefully in his wallet.

This is an interesting scenario. On the surface there appears to be little to worry about. Alan has found a part-time job which he says he enjoys and timekeeping has never been a problem at college. So what is happening that has put Alan in a potentially difficult position with his employment?

1. Tutor responsibilities

The tutor responsibilities are difficult to define here, because using a strict interpretation of educational boundaries you do not have a problem. Alan turns up on time for your sessions and he has found part-time employment. You could say that what happens outside of college is not your concern. And yet, within your role of being a tutor there is an implication, if not a stipulation, that you try and support learners, even if the presenting issues are outside of college. Only the most disciplined and stoical of learners will be able to leave their external baggage at the door of the classroom so that it does not interfere with their learning. The issues in this case study are created by Alan's number problems (see below). However, intervening with Alan's problems will not be easy as he may not even wish to acknowledge these problems. In this situation it is first important that Alan is supported to recognise he has number problems, which might involve a one-to-one tutorial where you try to bring to light these issues. This could be a lengthy process, and ultimately you will need to move to a position where you can persuade Alan to access specialist help and perhaps attend basic skills numeracy sessions.

2. Alan's number skills and coping strategies

There is little evidence in the case study to suggest what Alan's number skills are. This is because Alan has only poorly developed number skills. To compensate for this he has developed a range of coping mechanisms. Alan is late for work because he cannot tell the time and he does not have, nor does he intend to buy, a watch. Alan arrives at college on time because he starts to get ready for college as soon as he wakes up. He checks the time by asking the driver on the bus because even though he usually has his television on in the morning he cannot make sense of the digital clock on display. Although he does not catch the same bus each day, he catches one of a range of early buses that will get him to college on time. Alan is not late for his lessons in college because his friends accompany him and tell him when it is time to leave for the lesson. Alan has never had to learn to tell the time and he has learnt other strategies to help him to manage. Telling the time has never been a problem in the past because other people have always told him when to get up, when to go to school, eat his meals or go to bed. He was not late for lessons in school because a bell rang when he had to change lessons. However, now Alan is living independently, he needs to take responsibility for his own timekeeping. Because Alan has habitually relied on the support of others to help him through life he has been able to conceal his numeracy problems.

Alan also has problems with money. He understands that coins are low value and the notes are higher value, but he cannot relate the two. Alan does not understand that two 50-pence pieces have the same value as five 20-pence pieces, and that both are equivalent to one pound. Alan compensates for this by paying with notes whenever he can. That way he knows he will hand over enough money and he has delegated the responsibility of calculating the correct change to the assistant serving him, although in many stores such calculations are no longer performed by the assistant as most modern tills calculate the appropriate amount of change. Because Alan does not adequately understand currency he has difficulty in spending his loose change. Alan's coping strategy here is to save all his loose change in a jar until the jar is full, which he then takes to the change-convertor machine to receive more notes. Alan cannot complete this function himself and take the money to a bank because he cannot count and sort the coinage correctly. His other strategy is to ask the store cashier to take correct payment from the change he offers them, so avoiding the need to count and handle money himself. Over time Alan has learnt to camouflage and hide his number problems so that it appears that he does not need any support or help.

3. Alan's number problems

Alan's principal problem is his low level of number skills in all areas and he may even be dyscalculic. Consequently, he has become dependent on the kindness of others or on technology to help him compensate for his lack of skills. This is a fragile coping mechanism and it would only need tiny changes to upset the balance of Alan's life. If the coin-counting machine breaks Alan will have a cash flow problem; if his friends are off sick or he has a disagreement with them, no one will tell him it is time to go to lessons. When the clocks change from British summer time to Greenwich Mean Time, Alan will probably not wake early enough to catch one of his usual early morning buses and it is likely that he will be significantly late. As Alan does not appear to have developed a coping strategy to ensure he arrives punctually for his part-time work, an immediate concern is how Alan will manage to turn up on time for his evening job and avoid further disciplinary action or possible dismissal. And if Alan were to be dismissed, what would this mean for his short-term financial situation with less money available and higher shopping bills?

REFLECTIVE TASK

Consider the different learners you work and come into contact with. What do you know about their number skills and ability? Are there any indications that they are or could be experiencing problems involving number? In what ways could you positively intervene to support and help these learners with their problems?

Number skills and access to the economy

Building on the two case studies just outlined, consider how Sofia and Alan would access the economy. Sofia and Alan carry out most of their transactions using cash. However, this way of completing financial transactions is no longer the norm in many situations, and increasingly transactions are completed through credit arrangements. This does not just apply to high value purchases such as buying your home or a new car, but also to routine purchases including the weekly shopping or buying clothes. If you have a good credit rating it is likely you will easily be able to obtain a credit card to complete these purchases, as you represent a low risk to the credit card company, who will be confident they can recover their debt. Your credit rating is individual to you and is affected by factors such as the area where you live, the time which you have been at an address, whether you are in employment, any existing court judgements and your previous credit history. Cars and homes represent high-value purchases which many people need to secure finance for. However, for some sectors of the community, loans are necessary for much smaller purchases, like washing machines, televisions and school uniforms. If you are not in employment, securing finance for these lower-value items can be difficult. Because Sofia is on benefits, and has only been in her home for a short time, she currently has a poor credit rating. As a result of this credit rating it is unlikely Sofia will be able to secure a loan from a high street bank. Even if loan facilities were available in this way, most high street banks do not offer loans of hundreds of pounds, and minimum lending is usually around three thousand pounds. Although Sofia will probably have a bank account as most benefits are now paid directly into accounts, her financial status means it is unlikely her bank will be sympathetic to offering her an overdraft. Excluded from using bank loan facilities and unable to secure an overdraft, what options were available to Sofia that would not involve her paying 82 per cent interest to a doorstop moneylender?

It is possible that Sofia could have obtained the funds she needed by applying for a credit card. Even customers with poor credit histories can apply for credit cards and a number of companies specialise in assisting people with poor credit scores. Although interest rates from these types of companies are still high, at approximately 40 percent, they are significantly lower than those of doorstop lending. Credit cards can, however, be a problematic solution to a short-term cash flow problem. If used prudently they can ease cash difficulties. However, the inherent problem with credit cards is they represent money that can be accessed almost too easily. As most people tend to carry their credit cards with them at all times, they present the opportunity of spending money at almost any time on almost any item. If credit cards are used in this way, cumulative debts can soon build up, and customers can find themselves with a debt that they cannot service. In the worst case situations this leads to customers taking out another credit card to clear the debt of the first credit card. In this way credit card debt can soon spiral out of control and customers can accrue a debt of many thousands of pounds. A similar, and marginally less expensive option to a credit card, would have been to apply for a store-card and purchase Sam's uniform from a department store. Common rates of interest for store-cards are between 20 and 30 per cent. The disadvantage of a store-card is it ties you to one particular store or chain of stores. The advantage of a store-card is it can help to reduce the likelihood of accumulating large debts, as store-cards can only be used in named retail outlets and usually have a relatively low specified maximum spend.

A further option open to Sofia is she could have purchased Sam's uniform from a catalogue company. Purchases made this way are less convenient than cash or credit card purchases from shops. Although catalogues do not declare they add interest to their goods, items from catalogues are usually about a third more than you would expect to pay for a similar item purchased on the high street. The interest is effectively hidden in the cost of the goods. However, catalogues represent a realistic choice for low income groups as they allow customers to spread the cost of buying and paying back their debt over a period of time. Alternatively, if Sofia had any goods of significant value such as jewellery or electrical items, she could have used pawnbroking facilities. Pawnbrokers have, in recent times, seen a resurgence and have undergone a significant image change. Pawnbrokers have made concerted efforts to enter the mainstream economy and are no longer found in outlying districts or back streets, but are on the high street of many towns and cities. However, pawnbrokers continue to have an element of shame attached to them, and many people are reluctant to use their services. Interest rates between pawnbrokers differ, and vary between 6 and 20 per cent. Advances are usually for a period of six months, after which you can redeem your goods by repaying your loan with the relevant amount of interest or your goods will be sold on to recover the debt. If you are not able to redeem your goods and do not wish them to be sold, most pawnbrokers offer the option of arranging an extension on the existing loan.

There is little help available from the state for people in Sofia's position and, although the Department for Work and Pensions (DWP) has facilities to make crisis loans available to those on benefit, it is unlikely that Sofia would qualify for such a loan, as these loans are reserved for essential items such as cookers and bedding. While Sofia needs to buy Sam a uniform for school he does have other clothes that he can wear, and so it does not represent an emergency warranting state assistance.

A longer-term, more positive way for Sofia to secure finance would be for her to join a credit union. Credit unions are non-profit organisations that provide an alternative to banks. To be a member of a credit union you need to have a 'common bond' with other members of the union. This is usually achieved by all members living in the same area, although it could also be by working for the same employer or by some other bond. Members of credit unions save with the union, and can then borrow money from the union if they need to. The amount that each member is required to save varies between different credit unions but can be as little as £1 a week. By law credit unions cannot charge more than 2 per cent interest per month on a loan. Credit unions provide a cost-effective way for low income groups to access finance. A loan of £100 over 12 months, would therefore cost a maximum of £2 interest per month. This would mean that instead of paying £182 back to her money lender, Sofia would have only needed to repay £124 to the credit union.

A final avenue Sofia could explore to access finance is through the college she now attends. As a member of the college community Sofia would be able to gain help and support through the college welfare services. These services should be able to help Sofia to budget more effectively and might even be able to provide her with a non-repayable cash sum from student hardship funds which would help to ease her current financial difficulties.

Alan's options to access the economy are similar to Sofia as he is also in a low-income bracket. But because Alan does not have the same financial commitments as Sofia, he is not experiencing the same difficulties. Alan's limited number skills, however, still place him at risk of developing number-related problems, particularly in relation to finance and he would benefit from some form of financial counselling so he can avoid these problems in the future.

PRACTICAL TASK PRACTICAL TASK PRACTICAL TASK PRACTICAL TASK PRACTICAL TASK

Most colleges now have a range of different student support services. Investigate what types of financial support your college can provide – who is eligible and how learners can apply for assistance. How do you, or could you, promote these services so that your learners are aware of the different types of support available?

Number skills and employment

As the world of work has changed, so have demands on employees. In advanced economies there is now an increasing need for employees to have a higher level of skill in all areas, including number. Having underdeveloped number skills can cause significant difficulties and research has shown that *problems with numeracy lead to the greatest disadvantages for the individual in the labour market* and those with limited skills are *less likely to be employed, and if they are employed are less likely to have been promoted or to have received further training* (Smith, 2004, p13). Furthermore there is a *clear association between poor skills and economic inactivity* (Grinyer, 2005, p55). The need for number skills to gain and to retain employment has never been greater.

While the need for numeracy in *physical sciences, technology, business, financial services and many areas of ICT* (Smith, 2004, p11) is undisputed, it is important to recognise that regardless of the type of employment your learners hope to gain, they will need number skills. Virtually *all* forms of work in the current labour market require a degree of numeracy, although the specific level and type of number skills required will depend upon the employment chosen. Many traditional vocational jobs such as carpentry, plumbing and painting and decorating need a high level of number skills to carry out the role effectively. Employees need to be able to measure, understand angles, use volume, convert between different units of measurement and perform complicated calculations to complete work-related tasks. Indeed, if employees lacked these numerical skills their work would be substandard or dangerous, and they would be unlikely to keep their jobs. Equally, posts in service industries such as hairdressing, beauty and sports also need to use a wide range of number skills. Hairdressers need to calculate the different quantities of dye required to produce a particular tint, beauticians need to be aware of the temperatures on steam treatment machines and the safe temperature to apply waxes, while employees in sport and leisure may be required to work out safe exercise programmes for clients involving weights, times and sensible repetitions. The need for numeracy in employment has not lessened as employment has changed but increased, and employees in all kinds of roles are discovering that they need to be using and applying number skills to help them complete their work. Even in low-paid employment, number skills are needed, and Alan's current warehouse job requires that he uses skills to recognise number codes of products or select the correct number of boxes or pallets. However, with only limited numeracy skills Alan has little opportunity for advancement and if he wishes to progress he will need to gain more advanced numeracy skills.

The higher-paid professions such as medicine, law and accountancy have always assumed well-developed numerical skills, and it would be impossible to complete many aspects of these roles without appropriate numeracy skills. How could doctors determine the correct dosage level for drugs, or engineers calculate the load capacity of bridges or barristers work out financial wrongdoing in alleged fraud if they lacked appropriate number skills? Like Smith (2004), Grinyer (2005, p55) also found a link between numerical ability and employment and his work shows that those with *level 2 or above numeracy skills are less likely to be searching for work*, thus underlining the critical need for number skills in order to enter the labour market.

Unhelpfully, with the ready availability of technological aids, a modern myth has developed that numeracy *for the workplace has become less important* (Smith, 2004, p12). This was not true in the past, it is not true now and certainly will not be true of employment in the future. In order to offer employment many employers expect a certain level of numeracy and the government has set a national target, that the whole population needs to achieve at least level two numeracy skills (the equivalent of GCSE grade A*–C). Without these skills employment opportunities will be greatly reduced and those lacking number skills will be consigned to the fringes of society in low-status, low-paid employment with few opportunities for advancement

Awareness of technological and educational backgrounds

As society has changed over time we have become more reliant on technology. While this has produced many advantages it has also raised number-associated issues that need to be addressed. To an extent these issues are age-related and are different for older and younger adults.

Since the 1980s the availability and importance of technology in schools has increased. This has meant that many younger adults have developed a technological dependency where they rely on technological aids to assist them in solving all number problems. Because they have become reliant on using calculators for numerical problems they are unable to perform calculations without this support and are unfamiliar with simple numeric operations. They have not developed an awareness of number and do not realise how functions such as addition and subtraction, or multiplication and division are inversely related to each other. Nor do they appreciate the concept of multiplication being serial addition. Without an understanding of these ideas such learners lack the capacity to perform or check simple calculations they have completed. They are stuck in a 'the computer says' mentality and cannot operate without this support.

In contrast some older adults have developed a suspicion and distrust of technology as they are not accustomed to it. These adults would not consider using a calculator to perform calculations as they are more accustomed to mental arithmetic or using pen-and-paper methods. However, because of this technological distrust these same adults struggle to use cashpoints or self-service tills, preferring to be served by assistants. Other problems this group may experience are using digital microwaves, washing machines or programming DVDs or video recorders.

Both groups of adults are technologically disadvantaged, for while one group has become dependent on calculators, computers and other such devices and lacks basic numeracy skills, the other group has effectively excluded themselves from taking advantage of the benefits produced by technology as they cannot understand or else distrust technological innovations such as online banking, cashpoints and internet shopping.

A SUMMARY OF KEY POINTS

In this chapter we have explored:

> **the ways in which numeracy and number skills are embedded in our daily lives;**

> **the range of number skills needed to function effectively in different situations;**

> **the professional responsibilities of a tutor in supporting learners with number difficulties;**

> **how poor numeracy skills can lead to economic and social exclusion.**

These are difficult issues, and supporting learners to address the concerns they may face as a consequence of poor number skills is not a single-person job. It will only be possible to make a lasting difference by taking an integrated, multiagency approach, which helps to improve numeracy and understanding in a range of different arenas. There are no simple solutions or quick fixes to the problems that limited numeracy skills can cause. This single chapter could never hope to give each of these issues the attention it deserves; however, it will have served a useful function if it has helped to highlight the issues surrounding poor numeracy skills and indicated some of the ways in which you, as a tutor, can work to address these problems.

Learning review audit

Topic	I feel confident in doing this	This is an area I will need to develop
I can identify a range of situations in which my learners may encounter number		
I can specify the particular number skills that my learners might need to function in these situations		
I am aware of the support agencies they might need to use and I know how to contact these agencies		
I understand how number skills are integrated into my own subject specialist area		
I can provide opportunities for my learners to develop their number skills within my own subject specialist area		
I understand the relationship between employment opportunities and number		

REFERENCES   REFERENCES   REFERENCES   REFERENCES   REFERENCES

Crowther, G (1959) *15–18 A report of the Central Advisory Council for Education (England)*. London: HMSO.

DfES (2004) *Move on with a national qualification.* Nottingham: DfES Publications.

Grinyer, J (2005) *Literacy, numeracy and the labour market: further analysis of the skills for life survey.* Nottingham: DfES Publications.

Smith, A (2004) *Making mathematics count: report of Professor Adrian Smith's Inquiry into post-14 mathematics education.* London: HMSO.

Tout, D (2002) Introductory thoughts on numeracy. *Literacy across the Curriculumedia Focus*, 52: 9–11. Available at www.centreforliteracy.qa.ca

FURTHER READING   FURTHER READING   FURTHER READING   FURTHER READING

Cockcroft, WH (1982) *Mathematics counts: report of the committee of inquiry into the teaching of mathematics in schools.* London: HMSO.

Moser, C (1999) *Improving literacy and numeracy: a fresh start.* London: DfEE.

Websites

www.dfes.gov.uk/readwriteplus   ReadWritePlus
www.direct.gov.uk/geton   GetOn

6

Numeracy processes: performing calculations

By the end of this chapter you will be able to:

- recognise a variety of common errors in numeracy;
- understand some of the misunderstandings and misconceptions learners may have regarding numeracy;
- identify the methods and purposes of assessment in numeracy;
- describe the features of good and poor assessment.

Links to minimum core numeracy

A1   Awareness of misconceptions or confusions related to number-associated difficulties

A2   Awareness of methods and purposes of assessment in numeracy

Links to Professional Standards

CK 3.3   The different ways in which language, literacy and numeracy skills are integral to learners' achievement in own specialist area

EK 1.1   Theories and principles of assessment and the application of different forms of assessment, including initial, formative, and summative assessment in teaching and learning

EK 1.3   Ways to develop, establish and promote peer- and self-assessment

EK 2.2   Concepts of validity, reliability and sufficiency in assessment

EK 4.1   The role of feedback and questioning in assessment for learning

Links to Certificate in Teaching in the Lifelong Learning Sector (CTLLS)

Unit 2   Planning and enabling learning – demonstrate knowledge of the minimum core in own practice

Links to Diploma in Teaching in the Lifelong Learning Sector (DTLLS)

Unit 2   Planning and enabling learning – demonstrate knowledge of the minimum core in own practice

Unit 3   Enabling learning and assessment – how to apply minimum core specifications in own specialist area

Unit 4   Theories and principles for planning and enabling learning – how to apply minimum core specifications in own specialist area

Introduction

The way in which number skills are taught depends on:

- existing knowledge about teaching that skill;
- tutor preferences for teaching the identified skill;
- the learner's current understanding of the skill;
- contemporary 'fashions' in number teaching.

Different methods and approaches have been favoured over time and even now *there does not appear to be a 'best' method* (Frobisher et al, 2002, p143) to teach number skills.

The purpose of this chapter is to help you identify where learners may be experiencing problems and to suggest strategies that will help them overcome these concerns. Three principal areas will be considered.

- Errors in number work.
- Common confusions experienced by learners.
- Assessment in numeracy.

Errors in number work

All learners will make errors in their work. This should be expected. Making an error in itself is not necessarily a 'problem' and could simply be the result of a careless slip, which learners immediately recognise when it is highlighted. However, other errors may be indicative of a deeper misunderstanding on the learner's part, and can become a problem if this confusion is not addressed. In a busy working environment where there are competing priorities, it is tempting to simply provide learners with the correct answer. While this is feedback, inasmuch as it identifies an incorrect response, it may not help the learner understand why they have made an error or how this happened. Current teaching strategies encourage tutors to give *greater value and status to 'learning from mistakes' as a mechanism to assist further learning* (Drews, 2005, p14). To magically provide the correct answer in many ways merely serves to reinforce the mysterious nature of number and does not necessarily develop the learners' understanding.

To support your learners you will need to:

- find out what they were thinking when they attempted the problem;
- determine what processes they applied to solving the problem;
- understand how the learner approached the problem.

Simply reteaching the topic in the same way it was originally taught is not an adequate response. You need to find new ways to explain the concept to the learner. It is useful if you can persuade your learners to record how they arrived at a solution and to show their 'working-out'. This process will allow you to pinpoint where the error occurred and how the mistake was produced. This approach works well with learners who may be unwilling to engage in a conversation with their tutor. Alternatively you can take part in a learning discussion with your students to determine what they were thinking. This second strategy is particularly useful for learners who are reluctant to produce further written work and who find it easier to explain their thoughts verbally. Often, however, you will use a mixture of these two strategies.

Common confusions

This section reviews a range of number difficulties experienced by learners and provides useful insights into some of the more regularly presenting issues. Some confusions arise because learners do not understand how different skill areas are linked together. You can support learners by helping them to see *the ways in which the different operations are connected* so they can *make sensible judgements about how to use them* (Newmarch and Part, 2007, p5). Essentially, learners need to be aware of connections between number operations and, as an absolute minimum, should appreciate the interrelated nature of the four rules of number as shown in Figure 6.1.

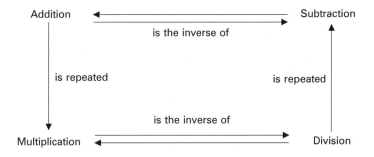

Figure 6.1 The four rules of number

Source: Newmarch and Part (2007, p5)

Five separate number skills are considered in this section – addition, subtraction, multiplication and division. Fractions, decimals and percentages are treated as a single interconnected skill area. For each area examples of incorrect learner calculations are provided for you to try and identify how the learner made the presenting error, followed by a review of the problems given.

Addition

After learners have developed the ability to count and have some understanding of the relative magnitude of numbers, one of the first number operations they are taught is addition. When learning to perform simple addition (single digits where no carrying is necessary) learners are often offered apparatus to help them understand how this process in completed. Once they are confident in this skill and as they progress to add larger numbers together, they may be introduced to written methods. A common method for this is shown below:

<table>
<tr><td>64
+48
112
1</td><td>In this method the learner begins by adding the smaller value figures in the units column first, working over to the higher value units, 'carrying' over any values necessary and allocating them to the correct column.</td></tr>
</table>

PRACTICAL TASK PRACTICAL TASK **PRACTICAL TASK** PRACTICAL TASK **PRACTICAL TASK**

Consider the following seven additions. Before reading the review provided afterwards try to work out what the learner was thinking in order to produce the answer given. What misunderstandings appear to exist in the learner's mind for each of the examples?

a	b	c	d	e	f	g
47	15	47	135	174	145	33 + 78 = 101
+16	+ 3	+ 16	+ 23	+ 28	+1724	
513	9	4176	58	192	21174	

Practical task review

Problem	Information learner understands	Information learner misunderstands	Strategies to assist
a 47 +16 513	Some understanding of traditional written method. Appreciates need to begin calculation in units column and has correctly added 7+6 to make 13, and 4+1 to make 5, but has not allocated these to correct columns.	Does not understand process of carrying 10 over to next column. Does not appear to understand place value. Does not recognise value of 5 in their answer as 500.	Use squared paper to help learner align numerals. Provide specific support on place value.
b 15 +3 9	Understands that numerals need to be added together to produce a total.	Does not understand the significance of place value or numeral position in a columnar addition and has simply added all the values together.	Learner needs to complete further work on place value. This could involve base 10 apparatus and/or place value cards.
c 47 +16 4176	Understands position where answer should be recorded.	Very little understanding apparent. Has not added any value to any other value, and so has not completed an addition calculation.	May need to be taken back to simple addition using physical apparatus before progressing onto more complex addition. May need further work using base 10 apparatus so can see comparative values of numerals.
d 135 +23 58	Understands process of columnar addition. Has applied correct process beginning with units column.	Has forgotten or overlooked need to add numerals in all 3 columns and has omitted to add in final 100.	Squared paper may help to keep learner focused and allow them to complete calculation in a methodical manner.
e 174 +28 192	Shows a good understanding of the processes required and is beginning to apply the correct procedures.	Has forgotten to carry 10 from units column to 10s column and so is unable to complete calculation correctly.	The learner may find it beneficial to use squared paper. Alternatively, the columns could be highlighted in different colours to help maintain focus.
f 145 +1724 21174	Understands numerals in columns need to be added together to produce a final sum. Understands where to record answer.	Calculation incorrectly laid out and figures not aligned in correct fashion. Does not appear to understand process of carrying and has entered 11 in answer space rather than carrying a value over.	Squared paper may support learner to set calculation out correctly. Support needed on producing estimated answers as a way of checking final answer is sensible.
g 33+78 =101	Learner has appreciated + is an instruction to add two values together. Learner understands their answer is to be recorded after = sign.	Learner has added 8 and 3 to produce 11 and has correctly entered 1 in their answer. Learner has forgotten to carry 10 along and so has incorrectly completed calculation.	Learner to be directed to use columnar approach to addition to avoid need to hold information in their heads.

Subtraction

Subtraction is often the next number operation that learners are taught. However,

> *there are procedural challenges to subtraction: subtraction is less intuitively obvious, there are distinct variations in meaning, and some of the elements of calculation, particularly when dealing with numbers with zeros, can be awkward to teach and difficult to learn.*

(Frobisher et al, 2002, p176).

As a result of these inherent difficulties many learners who may be comfortable and confident at performing addition work may struggle to complete subtraction calculations.

PRACTICAL TASK PRACTICAL TASK **PRACTICAL TASK** PRACTICAL TASK **PRACTICAL TASK**

Look at the following subtraction problems. Once again, try and identify where the learner has made an error, and why you think this occurred. If you were marking this learner's work what feedback would you provide and how would you give this?

$$
\begin{array}{llll}
a\ 424 & b\ \overset{1\,1}{424} & c\ \overset{2\,1\,1}{424} & d\ \overset{2\,9\,9\,9}{3000} & e\ \overset{1}{203} \\
-275 & -275 & -275 & -623 & -108 \\
\hline
251 & 259 & 59 & 2376 & 105
\end{array}
$$

Practical task review

Problem	Information learner understands	Information learner misunderstands	Strategies to assist
a 424 −275 251	Understands columnar layout. Understands one sum needs to be subtracted from the other. Appreciates need to begin calculation in units column.	Does not understand conventions to be applied in completing calculation. Does not understand figure in bottom row is to be subtracted from figure in upper row. Always subtracts smaller figure from larger figure regardless of position of numeral.	Conventions for completing subtraction sums need to be revisited. Concept of transferring values from one column to the next need to be developed.
b $\overset{1\,1}{424}$ −275 259	Understands principle of transferring values from one column to the next to enable calculation to be completed.	Does not understand need to reduce values in columns when transferring sums across and leaves original value unchanged. Thus the value of the figure they are subtracting from has been increased.	Needs to revisit conventions of value transfer. This could be supported by using base 10 apparatus.
c $\overset{2\,1\,1}{424}$ −275 59	Understands need to transfer amounts across to lower value columns to enable subtraction to be completed. Understands the need to reduce figure when transferring amounts to other columns.	Has not approached calculation in a sequential fashion and has transferred a value of 200 in a single step, allocating 100 to the 10s column and 100 to the units column (although this is now recognised as a transfer of 10).	Squared paper may help to keep learner focused and allow them to complete calculation in a methodical manner. Further work needed on transferring amounts supported by using base 10 apparatus. Learner needs to complete work on estimation.
d $\overset{2\,9\,9\,9}{3000}$ −623 2376	Understands it is not possible to subtract from zero and the need to transfer values across.	The presence of so many zeros have confused this learner. They have correctly recorded values for the first 2 transfers, but have become stuck in replicating 9 throughout the calculation.	This appears to be an oversight rather than a deep-seated misunderstanding. Further practice should help to address this concern.
e $\overset{1}{203}$ −108 105	Understands 8 cannot be subtracted from 3 so has attempted to transfer a value from the adjacent column. Although an incorrect procedure has been applied the learner has proceeded to complete the rest of the calculation correctly.	Has incorrectly transferred a value of 10 from a zero value.	Learner needs to complete further work on the significance of zero and the impact of zero in any given value.

Multiplication

This is the third number operation that learners are usually taught. Multiplication can be represented as a process of repeated addition. When discussed in this way learners may be happy to attempt multiplication problems. Although repeated addition will produce the correct answer there are other methods learners can use which will produce an answer more swiftly. It is once learners begin to attempt to complete long multiplication they sometimes begin to experience difficulties with this operation.

PRACTICAL TASK PRACTICAL TASK **PRACTICAL TASK** PRACTICAL TASK **PRACTICAL TASK**

Review the following three multiplication sums. Once again pinpoint where the learner has made an error, and why you think this occurred. What steps would you take to try and help this learner develop a deeper understanding?

$$a \quad \begin{array}{r} 24 \\ \times 16 \\ \hline 224 \end{array} \qquad b \quad \begin{array}{r} 24 \\ \times 16 \\ \hline 24 \\ +144 \\ \hline 168 \end{array} \qquad c \quad \begin{array}{r} 26 \\ \times 4 \\ \hline 122 \\ {\scriptstyle 4} \end{array}$$

Source: Spooner (2002, p25)

Practical task review

Problem	Information learner understands	Information learner misunderstands	Strategies to assist
a $\begin{array}{r}24\\ \times 16\\ \hline 224\end{array}$	Has correctly multiplied 6 × 4 to produce 24. Has correctly multiplied 10 × 20 to produce 200. However, the way they have recorded their answer indicates little understanding of all the processes involved in this calculation.	Does not understand process of completing long multiplication and has not multiplied all digits in turn. Does not appear to appreciate the significance of numeral position or place value. Does not understand process of carrying values over to next column.	Conventions for completing long multiplication need to be revisited, or alternative methods such as the rectangular sections method explored.
b $\begin{array}{r}24\\ \times 16\\ 24\\ +144\\ \hline 168\end{array}$	Has some awareness of multiplying numerals in bottom row by numerals in top row.	Has not understood that numeral 1, has a value of 10 and has incorrectly multiplied 1 × 24 to produce 24. Has incorrectly multiplied 6 × 24 to produce 144. Has incorrectly understood or only partly remembered process required. Does not understand process of carrying values.	The process for completing long multiplication needs to be revised, possibly beginning with multiplying a two-digit number by a single-digit number.
c $\begin{array}{r}26\\ \times 4\\ \hline 122\\ {\scriptstyle 4}\end{array}$	Understands bottom numeral must be used to multiply top numerals. Understands where answer should be recorded. Has some understanding of the need to carry numerals. Has correctly added all numerals in the 10s column, although has used the incorrect numerals.	Has incorrectly carried 4(0) instead of 2(0), and so cannot complete the addition.	Needs to have further practice on place value, possibly using base 10 apparatus.

For some learners, moving straight on to using a traditional pen-and-paper method to complete a long multiplication may be too challenging. For these learners the following two algorithms may be more accessible.

The rectangular sections method

This method involves learners using their knowledge of partitioning, and approaching the calculation as a series of smaller, separate calculations. An example of this method, for 28 × 34, is shown here.

×	20	8	600
			240
30	$30 \times 20 = 600$	$30 \times 8 = 240$	80
			+32
4	$4 \times 20 = 80$	$4 \times 8 = 32$	952

The first step is to split, or partition, each of the numerals, so that 28, is partitioned into 20 and 8. In the same way 34 is then partitioned into 30 and 4. Each of these numerals is then written on the horizontal and vertical sides of the rectangle. Four simpler multiplications are then completed in the grid. The last stage of the process is to add the totals of each of these calculations together to produce a final total.

Expanded notation method

This is similar to the rectangular sections method, and learners again have to partition the given numerals and complete a series of multiplications, before adding these totals together to produce a final answer.

$$
\begin{array}{rcl}
28 & = & 20 + 8 \\
\times\ 34 & = & 30 + 4 \\
\hline
30 \times 8 & = & 240 \\
30 \times 20 & = & 600 \\
4\ \times 8 & = & 32 \\
4\ \times 20 & = & +\ 80 \\
\hline
& & 952
\end{array}
$$

Division

Division is commonly the fourth number operation taught to learners. However, *many people find division difficult and confusing* (Newmarch and Part, 2007, p6). One of the difficulties contributing to this confusion is that division is sometimes taught in isolation from multiplication. This is not helpful for developing learners' understanding and it is important to *emphasise that each of these operations is the inverse of the other* (Newmarch and Part, 2007, p6). Such a strategy could help to avoid many early division misunderstandings.

PRACTICAL TASK PRACTICAL TASK **PRACTICAL TASK** PRACTICAL TASK **PRACTICAL TASK**

Look at the following division problems. What do you think the learner was thinking when they recorded their answers? How could you work with them to help them understand what they have done wrong and to help them avoid repeating this same error again?

a $\dfrac{13}{6\overline{)618}}$ b $\dfrac{101 \text{ r}2}{6\overline{)618}}$

Source: Spooner (2002, p28)

Practical task review

Problem	Information learner understands	Information learner misunderstands	Strategies to assist
a $\frac{13}{6\overline{)618}}$	Understands concept of divisor and dividend. Understands need to approach calculation in a sequential fashion. Understands need to carry 10 value over to 8 and read value as 18.	Has recorded position of 1 in their answer incorrectly. Has not appreciated need to record a zero between 1 and 3 indicating that 1 cannot be divided by 6 in this calculation.	Learner may be assisted by partitioning value given and asking 'how many 6s are there in 600?' to allow them to produce a rough estimate of final answer.
b $\frac{101 \text{ r } 2}{6\overline{)618}}$	Understands significance of divisor and dividend. Understands need to approach calculation in a sequential fashion.	Has viewed each digit in the value 618 individually – so has asked themselves, 'how many 6s in 6, how many 6s in 1 and how many 6s in 8?', rather than seeing figure as a whole.	Learner needs to view numbers holistically.

Fractions, decimals and percentages

Fractions, decimals and percentages can be considered to be equivalent expressions of the same concept. They are all ways of showing a proportion of a whole. Because of this it is useful to encourage learners to see them as alternatives, and to teach them as a complete package, enabling learners to make links between the three different forms of expression. A useful way of doing this is to present a chart of common fractions such as the one presented in Table 6.1 which shows decimal and percentage equivalents. Learners can be directed to view this as analogous with a currency exchange process, moving from euros, to dollars to pounds and while there may be different forms of expression, there is no loss in value.

Fraction	Decimal	Percentage
1	1	100%
$\frac{1}{2}$	0.5	50%
$\frac{1}{3}$	0.33	$33\frac{1}{3}\%$
$\frac{1}{4}$	0.25	25%
$\frac{1}{5}$	0.20	20%
$\frac{1}{10}$	0.1	10%

Table 6.1. Common fractions, decimals and percentages

Although this is a helpful teaching strategy, when learners use these skills they may experience different problems for each of the different skill areas. Consequently, they may require different forms of support to help them address any misunderstandings they have.

PRACTICAL TASK PRACTICAL TASK PRACTICAL TASK PRACTICAL TASK PRACTICAL TASK

Consider each of the five different problems below. What issues does each of these problems raise? What appears to be the misunderstanding in each example given? What strategies could you use to help learners resolve these misconceptions?

a $4\frac{2}{5} + 7\frac{3}{5} = 11\frac{5}{10}$ b $0.2 \times 100 = 20\%$ c $0.7 + 0.6 = 0.13$

d When asked to arrange the following series of decimals in ascending order beginning with the smallest a learner recorded the following response:

Original value	2.17	2.7	2.28	2.4	2.37	2.68
Learner's response	*2.4*	*2.7*	*2.17*	*2.28*	*2.37*	*2.68*

e A learner provided the following response when instructed to write the next three numbers in the series:

Original value	12.4	12.6	12.8	Learner's response	*12.10*	*12.12*	*12.14*

Source: Spooner (2002, problem c p23, problem d p21, problem e p22).

Practical task review

Problem	Presenting issues	Strategies to assist
a	• Does not recognise $^2/_5 + {}^3/_5 = 1$. • Believes top part of fraction and bottom part of fraction can be added independently. • Does not recognise $^5/_{10}$ as $^1/_2$ and has demonstrated an incomplete understanding of fractions.	May need to use practical apparatus to help them see how fractions relate to a whole and fractional equivalents.
b	• Has not read question correctly. Believes multiplying by 100 always means %. • Has not understood the question as a decimal multiplication.	Needs to revisit relationship between decimals and percentages.
c	• Learner has not understood the significance of the decimal place. • Learner has not understood how *deci*mal addition can produce numerals to the left and the right of the decimal place. • Has not understood significance of place value.	Needs to complete further work on place value, possibly using base 10 apparatus. Needs to use decimal number line to support understanding.
d	• Believes smaller numbers to be the same as fewer numerals. • Has not understood the significance of the decimal point.	Needs to use a decimal number line to help them understand how decimals function.
e	• Learner has recognised a familiar counting pattern and has reproduced this inappropriately. • Learner has not understood how the addition of 0.2 can change the figures to the left of the decimal place.	Needs to use a decimal number line to help them understand how decimals are arranged in sequence.

Assessment in numeracy

Assessment at all levels and in all sectors of education has taken on a heightened profile in recent years and *has a vital part to play in building (learners') understanding of mathematics* (Ofsted, 2008, p5). National government uses assessment data as a means of determining whether targets and goals have been achieved and learners use this and other data to help them choose which institution they will study in. Assessment is thus important on both a national and an individual scale.

There are many different definitions of assessment which can cause confusion over what the term actually means. Part of this difficulty is created by the different forms assessment can take. Black and Wiliam (2001, p2) define assessment as *all those activities undertaken by teachers, and their students in assessing themselves, which provide information to be used as feedback to modify the teaching and learning activities in which they are engaged.*

This definition is useful because it begins to uncover some of the main features of assessment. However, it neglects a key aspect of assessment, namely *what* is being assessed. Simplistically assessment in numeracy could be defined as a learner's ability to recall number facts or to apply given algorithms. For example, which times tables do they know, or can they complete long multiplication? However, assessment in numeracy needs to be about much more than simple facts or straightforward application – it should also be about determining a learner's ability to engage with unfamiliar and new situations. This requires learners to be flexible and to think creatively. By applying this model of assessment you can actively challenge learners to extend their understanding of the processes involved.

Purpose of assessment

Assessment is a process we undertake with learners to support their learning. While there is an ongoing debate regarding the essential purposes of assessment, it can be seen to have five principal functions. These are to:

- determine a learner's level of knowledge or understanding;
- identify any difficulties or problems the learner may be experiencing;
- establish the way in which learners understand processes and concepts;
- plan future teaching and learning activities;
- inform legitimate interested parties of current attainment levels (this may be reported individually or as an aggregate for a cohort or institution).

The prominence of each of these functions is significantly influenced by who require assessment to be completed. Learners (and their families) will be most interested in their own personal level of achievement; you as a tutor will want to know what learners understand (or not) so you can plan future learning activities; and college management teams and government bodies will be interested in collected attainment levels for groups and establishments. To this end the government also uses attainment data to produce the national league tables of colleges and schools.

Types of assessment

Roughly, three broad categories of assessment exist – diagnostic, day-to-day and periodic assessment. Although the processes used to complete assessment may be similar or even identical, the function of each type of assessment differs.

Diagnostic assessment can be used at any point during teaching to diagnose, or identify a learning issue. However, it is most commonly used at a natural start point before learners progress to or begin a new programme of study. Precisely assessing a learner's skills level is a detailed process which can be very time-consuming and may consist of a variety of different procedures including:

- reviewing records of previous achievements indicating level of attainment;
- screening to determine the learner's competence in numeracy, language, literacy and ICT;
- having detailed discussions with learners to find out their preferred approaches to learning;
- observing the learner while they study in order to determine how they like to work;
- marking learner work;
- providing subject-specific assessment material.

Once a detailed diagnosis of a learner's capabilities has been completed, you can then accurately direct learners to undertake appropriate courses which will benefit them. This may mean choosing between GCSE maths, key skills application of number, or a level 2 basic numeracy programme. The guidance you give to learners will depend on their individual skill level and how they intend to use the qualification. If diagnostic assessment has been carried out effectively it is likely you will be aware of the learner's future goals and motives for engaging in study. Although many of the processes applied in diagnostic assessment can be completed in an informal manner (for example, learner discussions) it is an essentially formal process used to accurately identify a learner's capabilities and capacity for learning at a given point.

Day-to-day or formative assessment, describes all the ongoing processes employed to collect evidence relating to a learner's understanding of mathematical processes, procedures and their current knowledge of key information. It swiftly provides information on learner achievement in each of these areas and can be used to inform future planning and teaching. Evidence collected in this way may be oral, written or observational. Tutors can use a variety of different strategies to collect this information including:

- short verbal answers;
- discussions with their learners;
- written question papers;
- quizzes or matching tasks;
- watching learners to see how they solve calculations.

Formative assessment can also include impressionistic data. However, such data should be treated with caution as it may be difficult to substantiate the validity of this type of information, and it will always need to be supported by the collection of more specific and verifiable data. Many of the processes used to collect evidence for day-to-day assessments are informal, although they can be punctuated with occasional formal tests or tasks.

Periodic or summative assessment occurs at the end of a set period of time or block of learning. This may be internally set by college tutors, or can be externally set by awarding bodies. Summative assessment checks learners' understanding of process, procedures and facts. Summative assessments are often written and may be carried out under controlled conditions. As such this type of assessment tends to be more formal. For summative assessment to be most use it needs to be reported back to both the learner and the tutor. While internally-set assessments can readily achieve this, some difficulties may arise with externally-set assessments, where often the only data provided is a final grade or mark. These data may be useful to the institution as a whole, but lacks the level of detail required by tutors and learners. Unless tutors and learners know exactly where their successes or concerns are, this information cannot easily be used to address individual learner difficulties or to maintain performance.

The use of ICT has become increasingly important in assessing learners and can be effectively used for diagnostic, day-to-day and periodic assessment. This could involve using a key skills numeracy screening programme, or might include an in-class quiz where learners use commercially produced software such as hand-held electronic voting systems to answer questions. These tools can be very useful as they protect learner anonymity and often the learners can receive instant feedback on their performance, indicating both successes and areas for further development.

All three main types of assessment can be supported by learners actively engaging in a process of self- and peer-assessment. Although you may be anxious about using these two approaches, fearful that some learners may be tempted to assess their own work too generously and that of their contemporaries too harshly, learners can become valuable partners in the assessment process. At the very least, there are usually many more learners in a class than there are tutors and sharing the responsibility for assessing work often increases the speed at which learners receive vital feedback. By encouraging learners to work cooperatively with each other, they can engage in a personal and group monitoring process, in which they consider their own and their colleagues' work and their personal achievement relative to their peers'. You can assist learners in becoming independent self-markers by providing them with checklists indicating what they should have learnt. However, you will still need to *apply some quality control* to help learners become *reliable judges of their understanding* (Ofsted, 2008, p49). While there are potentially many benefits to using peer- and self-assessment, some older learners struggle with this concept, preferring to recognise only the authority and expertise of the tutor. In this situation you need to work with learners to help them understand that the *most successful* (Ofsted, 2008, p48) learning environments provide opportunities for learners to assess their own and other learners' work, and it is this process which supports the development of deeper understanding.

REFLECTIVE TASK

Consider the following three 'mini-tests'. What do you identify as the benefits and disadvantages of each type of approach? Would you or could you consider using this form of assessment? Where and in what context do you feel it would be appropriate use this type of assessment?

Test A	Test B	Test C
3 + 6 =	☐ + ☐ = 14	☐ + ☐ =
9 + 8 =	☐ + ☐ = 21	☐ + ☐ =

Summary of the key features of good and poor assessment

Good assessment:	Poor assessment:
• Is evidentially based	• Is based on unsubstantiated views
• Is done *with* and *for* learners	• Is done *on* and *to* learners
• Uses a variety of different tools and approaches	• Adopts a single never-changing strategy
• Is developed over time	• Is a single snapshot in time
• Is completed in a planned fashion at regular intervals throughout the learning programme	• Is completed in a haphazard manner at sporadic intervals
• Directly feeds into the teaching process to inform future developments	• Is only used to produce data which does not relate to the teaching process
• Produces a holistic understanding of a learner's capabilities	• Produces an incomplete picture of learner abilities

PRACTICAL TASK PRACTICAL TASK PRACTICAL TASK PRACTICAL TASK PRACTICAL TASK

Numeracy assessments are often criticised for being dull and unimaginative, which provides little scope for learners to demonstrate their full ability. For your own subject area design a formative numeracy assessment task you could use with one of the groups you teach. Aim to integrate as many different numeracy skills as possible within this task.

A SUMMARY OF KEY POINTS A SUMMARY OF KEY POINTS

Learners need to have a good understanding of a variety of different number processes. The specific number processes they need will be influenced by the context in which they operate. However, all learners will need to have an understanding of certain basic number processes. Unfortunately, not all learners will have developed this understanding. This chapter has explored:

> some of the more frequent misconceptions and misunderstandings experienced by learners;

> possible strategies tutors can use to address these difficulties;

> the purpose of assessment in numeracy;

> ways in which number skills can be assessed.

You can support learners in developing their skills by working with them to assist them identify *where* and *why* errors have occurred. This process is complemented by promoting self- and peer-assessment so that learners eventually become involved in an ongoing learning dialogue in which checking and self-monitoring are an integral feature of the learning process.

Learning review audit

Topic	I feel confident in doing this	This is an area I will need to develop
I can identify common errors produced by learners		
I am able to appreciate the misunderstandings and misconceptions some learners may have regarding numeracy processes		
I understand the purposes and methods of assessment in numeracy		
I am able to embed opportunities within my own subject area to help learners develop their numeracy skills		

REFERENCES   REFERENCES   REFERENCES   REFERENCES   REFERENCES

Black, P and Wiliam, D (2001) *Inside the black box: raising standards through classroom assessment.* Available at ngfl.northumberland.gov.uk/keystage3ictstrategy/assessment/blackbox.pdf

Drews, D (2005) Children's mathematical errors and misconceptions: perspectives and the teacher's role, in Hanson, A (ed) *Children's errors in mathematics.* Exeter: Learning Matters.

Frobisher, F, Monaghan, J, Orton, A and Orton, J (2002) *Learning to teach number: a handbook for students and teachers in the primary school.* Cheltenham: Nelson Thornes.

Newmarch, B and Part, T (2007) *Maths4Life.* London: NRDC Publications.

Ofsted (2008) *Mathematics: understanding the score.* London: Ofsted.

Spooner, M (2002) *Errors and misconceptions in maths at Key Stage 2: working towards successful SATs.* London: David Fulton.

Surtees, L (2005) Handling data, in Hanson, A (ed) *Children's errors in mathematics.* Exeter: Learning Matters.

FURTHER READING FURTHER READING **FURTHER READING** FURTHER READING

Haylock, D and Cockburn, A (2006) *Understanding mathematics in the lower primary years: a guide for teachers of children 3–8.* London: Paul Chapman Publishing.

Parsons, R (ed) (2001) *Key Stage 3 mathematics: the revision guide.* Newcastle-upon-Tyne: Coordination Group Publications.

Websites

www.bbc.co.uk/skillswise   BBC Skillswise

www.bbc.co.uk/schools/gcsebitesize/maths   BBC Bitesize

www.gcse.com/maths   GCSE Maths Revision

www.mathsrevision.net/gcse/index.php   Maths Revision Net

7
Numeracy processes: presenting information

By the end of this chapter you will be able to:

- **support learners in making sense of number problems;**
- **assist learners in interpreting and evaluating their results;**
- **appreciate some of the issues associated with data representation;**
- **provide direction to learners to help them choose the most appropriate way to communicate their findings.**

Links to minimum core numeracy

A2   Knowledge of the capacity of numeracy skills to support problem solving

Ability to make sense of situations and to represent them

Role of interpreting results and drawing conclusions

Links to Professional Standards

CK 3.3   The different ways in which language, literacy and numeracy skills are integral to learners' achievement in own specialist area

CP 3.4   Ensure own personal skills in literacy, language and numeracy are appropriate for the effective support of learners

Links to Certificate in Teaching in the Lifelong Learning Sector (CTLLS)

Unit 2   Planning and enabling learning – demonstrate knowledge of the minimum core in own practice

Links to Diploma in Teaching in the Lifelong Learning Sector (DTLLS)

Unit 2   Planning and enabling learning – demonstrate knowledge of the minimum core in own practice

Unit 3   Enabling learning and assessment – how to apply minimum core specifications in own specialist area

Unit 4   Theories and principles for planning and enabling learning – how to apply minimum core specifications in own specialist area

Introduction

Numeracy provides the opportunity to communicate information clearly and succinctly. Data can be simply presented in graphs or charts, saving learners the challenge of producing large quantities of written prose. However, many learners have difficulty identifying where to begin when attempting to solve number problems and have even less idea on how they should present their work. The purpose of this chapter is to consider the different problem-solving skills needed by learners to engage with number work, and the skills they need to present their findings including:

- making sense of different situations and understanding problems;
- evaluating results produced;
- choosing how to report and communicate their findings to different audiences.

Problem-solving skills

Problem solving provides *the ideal opportunity to link mathematics to other areas of the curriculum and to the 'real world'* (Surtees, 2005, p127). As such it offers you, the tutor, scope to increase the relevance of the curriculum and to embed learning into real-life, everyday problems which learners may already have experience of, or are likely to encounter at some stage. It is in this way that numeracy begins to take on meaning for many learners and ceases to be an abstract disconnected exercise completed under protest or duress.

Sometimes it is the *everyday application of numeracy* (Newmarch and Part, 2007, p24) that learners find challenging, and it is problem solving that tests learners' ability to actually use number skills. Learners need to make appropriate decisions when using each of the three principal problem-solving skills described in the Introduction to this chapter and select the most suitable numeracy processes to apply to a given situation.

Learners will have different understandings of the three skill areas. As a tutor it is your function to impress upon learners how each of these skills is a facet of a whole and interconnected. Consequently, if their skills are weak in any one area, they may struggle to present sufficiently detailed work. On occasions number problems can be presented in a disaggregated way that only requires learners to demonstrate an individual problem-solving skill. For example, they may be supplied with some numerical data and will simply need to decide on the best method of communicating this information, ignoring the other skills of sense making and result evaluation. Even if this is the situation for your course, you still have a responsibility to ensure that learners develop their understanding of all three areas as you cannot be sure at what time or in what circumstances they may be required to use these skills.

Making sense of different situations

When working with learners, you may find it necessary to specifically teach them the problem-solving skills they need. This may involve instructing learners to systematically adopt the three-stage approach to problem solving illustrated in Table 7.1.

Stage 1: Understanding the problem	Stage 2: Deciding what to do	Stage 3: Looking back
Learners need to: • read the problem through carefully; • identify key words and check their meanings; • estimate what sort of answer to expect; • look carefully at the information given and decide what is relevant.		

Table 7.1 The three-stage approach to problem solving

Source: adapted from Newmarch and Part (2007, p25)

If learners begin calculations without taking time to consider what they have actually been asked to do, they can easily waste time completing lengthy calculations or other procedures which may have little relevance to the problem posed. Learners need to be encouraged to take a more considered approach to their work, and rather than hurrying to 'get started' need to be directed to use the three-stage model so that they fully understand the problem before beginning work.

Only once learners have understood the problem will they be able to make sensible decisions on what to do and how they should continue. It is at this stage that learners will need to make choices and select the processes needed to address the problem. This can be a confusing stage for learners, especially if they are fixed on the notion of a single 'right' solution. You may find it necessary to encourage learners to think flexibly and to generate a range of possible approaches before they decide which is the most appropriate.

REFLECTIVE TASK

How do you work with learners to develop their problem-solving skills? What approach do you currently adopt to help learners understand problems? Is there a particular model or method you advise learners to use when tackling problems? How effective is your current method and is there any way it could be improved?

Evaluating results produced

An important part of the three-stage approach to problem solving is using checking strategies to confirm if the answer provided is sensible. Even before starting work learners should use their existing knowledge to help them suggest a likely answer or possible solution. By using estimation strategies, such as rounding, learners can save themselves time and effort, allowing them more opportunity to concentrate on producing high-quality, well-presented work. Learners should use their judgement on the degree of accuracy required by the problem, and may need to be persuaded that in some circumstances it is sufficient to use approximation strategies to reach a solution. The degree of precision is dependent on the problem posed and learners need to become comfortable with using the idea of using 'mathematical short cuts' in some situations. For example, if you ask learners whether £10 will be enough to pay the bill in a burger bar for a group of friends, when the individual spend for each person was £2.80, £3.60, £3.49 and £2.11, learners need only add the whole pounds to be able to provide an answer. It is not necessary to say how much more the bill will come to, and learners need not waste time completing exact calculations including pence.

Self-checking is an important step in becoming an autonomous learner. Rather than relying on you, the tutor, as their first point of reference, learners should be encouraged to employ a range of personal-monitoring processes to determine whether or not the solution they have suggested makes sense. By promoting this independence you will provide your learners with the opportunity to develop a greater sense of number awareness and consequently they will *only need to refer to (you) once they have explored all other options* (Newmarch and Part, 2007, p27).

Initially learners may need guidance on how they should check their work. You can support learners here by suggesting possible strategies that they might use. These could include:

- asking learners to try different methods to see if they still produce the same solution;
- explaining their work to another learner;
- reviewing similar work they may have completed previously;
- using reference material to check number facts;
- discussing their work with other learners in the group.

At this stage of problem solving, learners should review the processes they used to solve the problem. You can help learners here by providing them with a standard bank of questions to evaluate the effectiveness of the procedures used. These might include:

- was their final solution similar to the predicted outcome?
- were they able to use any legitimate 'shortcuts'?

- how clearly had they communicated their findings?
- what forms of graphical presentation could they/did they use?
- in what ways could their solution be improved?

By encouraging learners to become self-evaluative, reflective problem solvers, you will further develop learner independence and enable them to begin to use their numeracy skills in everyday real-life contexts.

REFLECTIVE TASK

What benefits can you (and your learners) identify in using checking strategies? What range of checking strategies do you currently encourage your learners to use? Of these strategies which ones have learners found most useful? How could you work with your learners to ensure that they systematically use self-checking strategies?

Communicating findings

The choice of *how* to represent information can be a difficult decision for learners. This may result in learners making inappropriate choices such as using a line graph when a bar chart would be more suitable or producing a pie chart when a simple table would suffice. These poor choices may result from an incomplete understanding of the principles associated with different forms of representation (for example, line graphs are not suitable for representing discontinuous data) or could simply be because the learner only knows how to construct one sort of chart. To enable learners to produce the best work they can, you may need to teach them how to construct different types of chart, and the conventions relating to each form. Only once learners understand these processes will they be able to make good decisions on the form of representation to use.

The purpose of using charts, tables and graphs must always be to facilitate communication and *often data presented graphically (is) easier to comprehend* (Orton and Frobisher, 1996, p149). As such, graphs and charts are a good means to convey information, but it is important that learners are able to use them *clearly, accurately and attractively* (Orton and Frobisher, 1996, p149).

Table 7.2 provides a summary of the types of graphs and charts learners most commonly need to use and the purposes for which they are most suited.

Type of chart or graph	Type of data suitable for
Bar charts	These are suitable for representing discrete, discontinuous data. The discontinuous nature of the data is further made apparent by the spaces between the bars. Both axes should be clearly labelled. Apart from exceptional circumstances any numerical scale used should increase incrementally by equal amounts.
Line graphs	Line graphs are suitable for showing continuous data. The independent variable is shown on the horizontal axis (for example time, or months of the year) and the dependent variable is shown on the vertical axis (for example temperature). Points on the graph are joined, emphasising that both the given points and the intervals between the points have meaning.

Pie charts	Many learners find these charts difficult to construct by hand although a simple, low cost, hand-held pie chart-making tool is now available. Alternatively, there are many computer programmes that can be used to produce these charts. Pie charts are visually attractive and are particularly useful for showing the various proportions of categories. The usefulness of pie charts becomes questionable when there are numerous categories within a set and this form of representation is best limited to smaller numbers of categories.
Scatter graphs	These are very useful for linking two variables, for example, age and height of learners. Once learners have plotted all their points, they should draw a line of best fit, to show trends within the data.
Pictograms	These can be a fun way for learners to represent data and may be a used as a step to helping learners construct bar charts. Care may need to be shown in using this form of data representation, as some learners may perceive it to be a childish format. Pictograms are best suited to discontinuous data. Each picture chosen is given a numerical value – for example, a single car may be chosen to show 10 journeys to work. However, learners may struggle to accurately reproduce multiple images and may need to be advised to choose simple pictures or to use computer software to generate appropriate imagery. Difficulties can arise where learners may need to show part of an image to represent a fraction of the chosen numerical value. How, for instance, would a learner show seven car journeys?
Tables	This is often an initial step in the data collection process. Tables can be useful as they provide a means of collating large quantities of data in one place. While it is often necessary for learners to collect information in this form, they need to decide whether this is the best way to show information in their final work.

Table 7.2 Types of charts or graphs and purposes for which they are suited

REFLECTIVE TASK

Consider the following two different forms of data representation. What observations do you make about the ease with which the data can be understood? What circumstances can you identify where graphical representation would be more suitable than tabular information, and when do you consider it better to use tables rather than graphs?

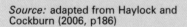

Achievement level in numeracy	Number of learners
Entry 1	3
Entry 2	6
Entry 3	12
Level 1	10
Level 2	12

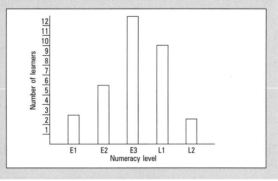

Source: adapted from Haylock and Cockburn (2006, p186)

Problem solving in practice

Problem-solving activities provide rich opportunities for learners to engage in number work on a variety of different levels and to practise all three problem-solving skills. The following two problems illustrate the types of situations your learners may encounter and the skills they will need to address problems like these.

Problem – planning a family gathering

You have asked learners to plan catering for a family gathering of 16 people – two senior citizens, seven adults over 18, four teenagers and three children aged 5–10 for a given budget. You have chosen not to be prescriptive in the way learners approach this work as you want them to have the opportunity to show how well they can solve the problem. You have told the group that, should they feel they are having difficulties, you are able to offer help. By the end of the project you have directed learners to submit a report which details:

- their plan for addressing the problem;
- information on how they reached their decisions;
- their proposed solution;
- how they checked their calculations to show they made sense;
- ways in which they think they could improve their chosen solution;
- how they ensured that they stayed within budget.

While all learners will be able to engage with this work, an open-ended project like this provides for differentiated outcome by results, where the most able and well-motivated learners will be able to produce an extended final piece and where the least competent learners can supply a basic solution to this problem.

Discussion

The actual data provided in this example is limited – learners have only been told the size of the group, the age range of the party and the budget available to spend. Because this problem is contextually based on a real-life situation many learners will be able to readily relate to this example. However, before learners can make sense of the problem posed, they will have needed to answer a number of general questions. For example, will they provide the same food for all guests regardless of their age? Will they prepare a hot meal or cold snacks? Do they need to consider any special dietary requirements? While these questions may not be mathematically based, learners need to engage in this thinking process so that their finished project has real meaning and so that their final suggestions are coherent.

Once learners have answered these preliminary questions they would have needed to employ a variety of different numeracy skills to address the primary problem. In determining the different quantities of foods needed, most learners would have used:

- budgeting skills to determine the best value purchases;
- multiplication skills where they have purchased multiples of the same item;
- addition skills to calculate the final total.

Some more able learners may have decided to produce an in-depth piece of work and will have included a time schedule indicating the sequence for preparing the food so that it is ready in time for the gathering.

The principal evaluation skill used by learners is to ensure the project has remained within budget. However, some learners may have extended this by providing a cost comparison across different stores showing the most expensive and cheapest providers. If learners have exceeded the given budget, they should have revisited their plan and made decisions on what to leave out, determining where and how savings could be made. Learners should be instructed to check calculations by completing the appropriate inverse operation or by using some other checking process.

The final report produced by learners will depend on how they approached the task. However, for a problem of this nature it is likely most learners would submit written prose accompanied by their cost calculations. Some learners may also include graphs or charts to show the relative costs of items.

Problem – tiling a bathroom

For this project you have instructed learners to calculate the cost of tiling a bathroom. They need to tile the wall above the bath and above the sink. You have not given them a specific budget but have directed them to produce a good quality job while keeping the final cost of the project as low as possible. Learners should choose what type of tiles to use, the height to which they will tile and decide if any additional purchases are necessary. On completion of the project you have told learners to submit:

- detailed calculations showing how they worked out the number of tiles required;
- information on how they checked their calculations to show they made sense;
- plans and/or diagrams showing the way they tiled the bathroom;
- calculations showing the overall cost of the project;
- a project evaluation indicating where they could make improvements to their work.

Discussion

This example is another open-ended project in which learners can demonstrate a variety of skills. There are less preliminary non-mathematical decisions needed by learners, and they can quickly begin to make sense of this problem by calculating the total area to be tiled by using relevant formulae to determine area. Learners should have determined the total number of tiles needed for the project by using division skills, and, by multiplying the total number tiles with the unit price, calculated the cost of materials needed. Finally by adding the cost of other additional items such as adhesive and grout, learners would have been able to produce an overall cost for the project.

In evaluating their results learners would have needed to consider where potential savings were possible. This might have been by reducing the height to which they tiled. At this stage learners would have needed to apply appropriate checking mechanisms to make sure the results produced made sense, for it is often in making modifications that learners can make errors. Projects involving area are well suited to computer modelling techniques, and where this facility is available you should consider asking learners to use this support to help them explore the problem.

In submitting their final report learners should have been encouraged to provide scale or sketch diagrams, showing how they arrived at their solution, together with their calculations indicating costs.

PRACTICAL TASK PRACTICAL TASK PRACTICAL TASK PRACTICAL TASK PRACTICAL TASK

Either by yourself or with a colleague, devise a practical, subject-specific numeracy problem-solving activity for your learners. Aim to produce a problem that will give learners an opportunity to use a wide range of numeracy skills that would also be accessible to all learners regardless of skill level.

Effective teachers of numeracy

Successful teachers of numeracy find ways to make number work meaningful, relevant and enjoyable. They make learning a rewarding rather than a painful process and support learners to achieve by working collaboratively with them to attain agreed, negotiated goals. To be a successful numeracy tutor you should:

- be competent in using numeracy within the context of your own subject;
- be able to demonstrate the interconnected nature of number operations to your learners;
- show a wide awareness of different number processes;

- work collaboratively with your learners to help them identify the most appropriate methods for a given situation;
- provide clear verbal explanations of processes and algorithms, possibly supported by other written materials;
- develop the ability to explain the same concept in a variety of different ways;
- recognise learner achievement and reward this appropriately;
- provide opportunities for students to learn through discovery;
- support learners to believe in their capacity to be numerate;
- keep up to date with your own professional development.

Through displaying these qualities you will be able to empower learners to become independent self-supporting students, with the ability to solve numeracy problems in both familiar and unfamiliar situations.

A SUMMARY OF KEY POINTS A SUMMARY OF KEY POINTS

This chapter explored:

> **how tutors can work with learners to help them make sense of different number problems;**

> **the different checking strategies learners can use;**

> **appropriate ways learners can communicate their findings;**

> **some examples of contextualised numeracy problems.**

Number and mathematics have traditionally been taught as a separate subject area. This model of teaching has not been entirely successful and the disaggregated way number has been taught has partly contributed to the low levels of achievement seen today, in which many learners have compartmentalised number skills viewing them simply as 'something they did at school'. If the population as a whole is to become more numerate a new approach to teaching numeracy is required. The examples provided earlier in the chapter show how number can be embedded in different ways so that it has greater relevance. Number work needs to be integrated into *all* subjects, in *all* areas of study and in essence delivered both covertly by stealth, as well as overtly through more traditional mechanisms. Colleges and training organisations have the opportunity of being at the forefront of providing truly integrated numeracy opportunities for learners and to develop learners' skills through contextualised number problems. In this way learners can be exposed to real-life number problems and can develop their skills through both integrated and discrete study opportunities.

Learning review audit

Topic	I feel confident in doing this	This is an area I will need to develop
I am able to support learners to make sense of different number problems		
I can provide guidance to learners on selecting the most appropriate way to communicate their findings		
I can assist learners in interpreting and evaluating the results they produce		
I am able to provide contextualised learning opportunities within my own subject area, to help learners develop their numeracy skills		

REFERENCES REFERENCES REFERENCES REFERENCES REFERENCES

Haylock, D and Cockburn, A (2006) *Understanding mathematics in the lower primary years: a guide for teachers of children 3–8.* London: Paul Chapman Publishing.

Newmarch, B and Part, T (2007) *Maths4Life.* London: NRDC Publications.

Orton, A and Frobisher, L (1996) *Insights into teaching mathematics.* London: Cassell.

Surtees, L (2005) Handling data, in Hanson, A (ed) *Children's errors in mathematics.* Exeter: Learning Matters.

FURTHER READING FURTHER READING FURTHER READING FURTHER READING

Lawler, G (2007) *Understanding maths: basic mathematics explained.* Abergele: Studymates.

Mainwaring, G (2006) *Adult learners' guide to numeracy.* Edinburgh: Chamber Harrap.

Potter, L (2006) *Mathematics minus fear.* London: Marion Boyars.

Websites
www.bbc.co.uk/skillswise/numbers/handingdata   BBC Skillswise
www.bbc.co.uk/schools/gcsebitesize/maths/data   BBC Bitesize

A final word

Thank you for taking the time to read all, or part, of this book. I hope you found it useful in some way. This book is not the first, nor the last word, on numeracy teaching and supporting learners. There are many other texts, journals, websites and articles that you may find it helpful to explore. However, it will have achieved a useful function if it has given you the opportunity to think about how you feel about number, how your learners might feel about number, the significance of number in society and the impact that number can have on our own and our learners' life experience. Big issues are never simply or easily addressed, but issues are never addressed unless we can begin to engage with them. Hopefully this book has been the start (or the continuation) of that process.

Appendix 1
Glossary of acronyms

Below is a list of the abbreviations used within this text. There are many more acronyms and abbreviations within the lifelong learning sector and you may need to check these, using a suitable search facility on the internet.

ALG	Adult Learning Grant
ASC	Autistic Spectrum Conditions
ASD	Autistic Spectrum Disorders
ATLS	Associate Teacher Learning and Skills
BSL	British Sign Language
CPD	Continuing Professional Development
CSE	Certificate of Secondary Education
CSW	Communication Support Worker
CTLLS	Certificate in Teaching in the Lifelong Learning Sector
DDA	Disability Discrimination Act
DfEE	Department for Education and Employment
DfES	Department for Education and Skills
DIUS	Department for Innovation, Universities and Skills
DTLLS	Diploma in Teaching in the Lifelong and Learning Sector
DWP	Department for Work and Pensions
GCE	General Certificate of Education
GCSE	General Certificate of Secondary Education
ICT	Information Communication Technology
IfL	Institute for Learning
ILEA	Inner London Education Authority
ILP	Individual Learning Plan
LLUK	Lifelong Learning UK
NAO	National Audit Office
NCETM	National Centre for Excellence in Teaching Mathematics
NIACE	National Institute of Adult and Continuing Education
NNS	National Numeracy Strategy
Ofsted	Office for Standards in Education
PDA	Pathological Demand Avoidance
PGCE	Professional/Post-Graduate Certificate in Education
QIA	Quality Improvement Agency
QTLS	Qualified Teacher Learning and Skills
SfL	Skills for Life
SfLIP	Skills for Life Improvement Programme
SMOG	Simplified Measure of Gobbledegook
TIMSS	Third International Mathematics and Science Study
U3A	University of the Third Age

Appendix 2
Summary of The Minimum
Core for Numeracy requirements

Personal, social and cultural factors influencing numeracy learning and development

- The different factors affecting the acquisition and development of numeracy skills.
- The importance of numeracy in enabling users to participate in, and gain access to, society and the modern economy.
- Potential barriers that hinder development of numeracy skills.
- The main learning difficulties and disabilities relating to numeracy skills learning and development.
- The common misconceptions and confusions related to number-associated difficulties.

Explicit knowledge of numeracy communication and processes

Communication
- Making and using decisions about understanding.
- Communicating processes, and understandings.

Processes
- A knowledge of the capacity of numeracy skills to support problem solving.
- Making sense of situations and representing them.
- Processing and analysis.
- Using numeracy skills and content knowledge.
- Interpreting and evaluating results.
- Communicating and reflecting on findings.

Personal Numeracy Skills

Communication
- Communicate with others about numeracy in a open and supportive manner.
- Assess own, and other people's, understanding.
- Express yourself clearly and accurately.
- Communicate about numeracy in a variety of ways that suit and support the intended audience, and recognise such use by others.
- Use appropriate techniques to reinforce oral communication, check how well the information is received and support understanding of those listening.

Processes
- Use strategies to make sense of a situation requiring the application of numeracy.
- Process and analyse data.
- Use generic content knowledge and skills.
- Make decisions concerning content knowledge and skills.
- Understand the validity of different methods.
- Consider accuracy, efficiency and effectiveness when solving problems and reflect on what has been learnt.

- Make sense of data.
- Select appropriate format and style for communicating findings.

LLUK (2007) *Addressing literacy, language, numeracy and ICT needs in education and training: defining the minimum core of teachers' knowledge, understanding and personal skills* pp58–59.

Index

Please note: the letter 'f' following a page number refers to a figure; the letter 't' refers to a table.